SUCCESS JOURNAL FOR WOMEN

SUCCESS COMES FROM YOU

DISCOVER THE FEMALE POWER
YOU POSSESS WITHIN

ANGELA YOUNG

Table of Contents

PART 1 5

Chapter 1: 6 Ways To Adopt New Actions That Will Be Beneficial To Your Life.. 6

Chapter 2: Be Inspired to Create... 11

Chapter 3: 10 Habits to Change Your Life.. 13

Chapter 4: How to Learn Faster.. 20

Chapter 5: How Getting Out of Your Comfort Zone............................ 23

Chapter 6: 7 Habits To Change Your Life 26

Chapter 7: Creating successful habits. 31

Chapter 8: 7 Ways To Discover Your Strengths 36

PART 2 42

Chapter 1: 7 Habits That Are Good For You.. 43

Chapter 2: 10 Habits That Make You More Attractive 48

Chapter 3: 10 Habits That Damage Your Brain 55

Chapter 4: 8 Steps To Develop BeliefsThat Will Drive you To Success 60

Chapter 5: 7 Habits of Healthy Relationships....................................... 66

Chapter 6: Stay Focused. 71

Chapter 8: How To Succeed In Life.. 78

PART 3 87

Chapter 1: *How To Stop Wasting Time*... 88

Chapter 2: How To Share Your Talent.. 92

Chapter 3: How to Reprogram Your Mind for Success 95

Chapter 4: How to Acknowledge The Unhappy Moments?.................. 99

Chapter 5: Five Steps to Clarify Your Goals.. 103

Chapter 6: 6 Habits of Oprah Winfrey... 108

Chapter 7: 6 Concerning Effects of Mood On Your Life.................... 112

Chapter 8: 5 Ways To Adopt Right Attitude For Success.................... 117

Chapter 9: Don't wait another second to live your dreams.................. 121

PART 1

Chapter 1:
6 Ways To Adopt New Actions That Will Be Beneficial To Your Life

There is this myth that goes around saying that, once you leave your teenage, you can never change your Habits. One can analyze this for themselves. Everyone has a list of new year's resolutions and goals. We hope to get these things done to some extent, but, never do we ever really have a clear idea of how to get to those goals in the least possible time.

We always desire a better future but never really know how to bring the necessary change in our lives. The change we need is a change in attitude and behavior towards life altogether. Change is never easy, but it is achievable with some sheer willpower. You might be on the right track to lead a better life, but there are always more and better things to add to your daily habits that can be helpful in your daily life.

Here are 6 simple yet achievable actions you need to take:

1. **Decide Today What Is Most Important In Your Life**

Life is a constant search for motivation. The motivation to keep doing and changing for the better. Once you have something to change for, take a moment and envision the rest of your life with and without the change you are about to make.

If you have made up your mind, now think about how you can start off with these things. For starters, if you want a healthy lifestyle, start your day with a healthy breakfast and morning exercise on an empty stomach. If you want to scale your business, make a customer-friendly business model.

2. **Make Reasonable and Achievable Goals.**

Adopting new habits can be challenging, especially if you have to change something in your day-to-day life to get better results. Start easy by making goals that are small, easy, reasonable, and won't give you a headache.

You can start off with baby steps. If you want to become more responsible, mature, and sorted in your life, just start your day by making your own bed, and do your dishes. Ride a bicycle to work, instead of a car or a bus. Things become smooth and easier once you have a reason for the hard acts.

3. **Erase Distractions from Your Daily Life**

You have wasted a lot already, don't waste any more time. As young as you are right now, you should feel more privileged than the older people around you. You have got the luxury of time over them. You have the right energy and pinnacle moments to seize every opportunity you can grasp.

Don't make your life a cluster of meaningless and profit-less distractions. You don't have to go to every public gathering that you are invited to. Only those that give you something in return. Something that you can avail yourself of in your years to come. Don't divulge in these distractions only for the sake of memories. Memories fade but the time you waste will always have its imprint in every moment that follows.

4. Make a Diary and a Music Playlist

You can devote some time to yourself, just to communicate with your brain and start a discussion with yourself. Most people keep a diary for this purpose, some people tend to make a digital one these days. When you start writing to yourself in the third person, talking and discussing your issues and your weaknesses, you tend to find the solutions within.

Most people find it comforting and calming when they have a playlist of music playing in the background while working. Everyone can try this to check if they get a better level of creativity if they have some small activity that soothes their stressed nerves.

5. Incorporate Regular Walk and Exercise in Your Life

When you know you have a whole day ahead of you, where you have to sit in an office chair for the next 8 hours. Where you have to sit in your home office looking at those sheets for most of the day. A 10 min walk before or after the busy schedule can help a lot in such conditions. You can never avoid physical activities for your whole life, especially if you want to live a healthier and longer life.

People always feel reluctant to exercise and running once they enter college or work life. Especially once they have a family to look out for. But trust me, your body needs that blood rushing once a day for some time. You will feel much more pumped and motivated after a hard 2-mile jog or a 15 min workout.

6. Ask Others for Help and Advice

You have a life to live for yourself, but always remember, you are never too old to ask for help. A human can never perfect something in their life. You will always find someone better than you at a particular task, don't shy to ask for help, and never hold back to ask for any advice.

We feel low many a time in our lives. Sometimes we get some foul thoughts, but we shouldn't ever pounce on them. We should rather seek someone's company for comfort and sharing our concerns.

Conclusion

The ultimate success in life is the comfort you get at the end of every day. Life can never be fruitful, beneficial, and worth living for if we don't arrange our lives as resourceful human beings. Productive minds always find a way to counter things and make the best out of everything, and this is the art of living your life.

Chapter 2:
Be Inspired to Create

Some of you will look in the mirror today and think that you are weird. You will see that you are different to other people. That you are quirky or odd. But I want to encourage you. Not only is your uniqueness something that you should embrace but it is perhaps your greatest asset. The wonderful thing about people being different is that they think a little differently, see the world from a slightly different perspective. The combination of the various bits of knowledge that they have fit together in different ways.

When you speak you are most likely not conscious of your accent. Maybe if you live in a foreign country you are hyper aware of it. But how many of you know that your mind has an accent too. It has an accent that is formed from your experiences. Your experiences with pain. Your experiences with joy. Your experiences with success, failure and even your experiences with the everyday mundane. Not only that but the accent of your mind constantly evolves.

Why does that matter?

Because it is that accent which enables you to innovate. When you speak a foreign word, it takes on a new form in your accent – sometimes it may even be a sound that has never been uttered with that tone and inflection. It is completely original not because of the form of the word but because of the accent that informs the way the word comes out.

The same is true of your mind. You can speak the same ideas, study the same fields, even research the exact same thing and still end up with different outcomes. How? Because your outcomes are being informed by your experiences. Your ideas are your present thoughts running rampant through familiar thought patterns. They are tailored towards a particular style. For some of you it is like your mind rolls the r's in your ideas. It adds a certain *je ne sais quoi* to your ideas. To others your accent is thick and mutes the aesthetic nuances of ideas – manifesting in wonders of logic and mechanics.

Whatever it may be, I encourage you to embrace the accent of your mind. Actually, I demand you to. It is time that you stopped denying the world of your contribution to it. It's time that you got inspired to create. It is time that you allowed ideas to implode within the realm of your consciousness and innovations to pour out of it. Whether you find your language in art, dance, engineering, or politics. If you have a niche area of knowledge or see a pattern from a unique combination of information then it is about time you harnessed that and rode the creation train to wherever it may take you. I can promise you that you will never look back. We tend to regret the things we did not do, not the things that we did.

Listen closely and hear the accentuation of your thoughts. Then speak their creative ingenuity into being.

Create something that only you can.

Chapter 3:
10 Habits to Change Your Life

I'm sure everyone wonders at a certain point in their life that what is the thing that is stopping them from reaching their goals. It is your bad and unhealthy habits that hold you down. If you want to succeed in life, you need to get rid of these habits and adopt healthy habits to help you in the long run.

Here are 10 healthy habits that will change your life completely if you can adopt them in your daily life:

1. Start Following a Morning Ritual

Everyone has something that they love to do, i.e., things that boost their energy and uplifts their mood. Find one for yourself and do that every morning. It will help you kickstart your day with a bright and cheerful mood. It will also help you to eliminate mental fatigue and stress. You will find yourself super energetic and productive. Let me tell you some morning rituals that you can try and get benefitted from.

- *Eating Healthy:* If you are very passionate about health and fitness, eating healthy as a morning ritual might be a win-win situation for you. You can have a nutritious breakfast every morning. Balance your breakfast with proper amounts of carbs, fats, proteins, etc. It will not only help you in staying healthy but will also help you kickstart your day on a proactive note.

- *Meditating:* Meditation is an excellent way of clearing your mind, enhancing your awareness, and improving your focus. You can meditate for 20 to 30 minutes every morning. Then you can take a nice warm shower, followed by a fresh cup of coffee. Most importantly, meditating regularly will also help you strengthen your immune system, promote emotional stability, and reduce stress.

- *Motivating:* A daily dose of motivation can work wonders for you. When you are motivated, your productivity doubles, and you make the best out of your day. Every morning, you can simply ask yourself questions like, "If it is the last day of your life, what do you want to do?", "What productive thing can I do today to make the best out of the day" "What do I need to do in order to avoid regretting later for having wasted a day?". When you ask yourself questions like these, you are actually instructing your brain to be prepared for having a packed-up and productive day.

- *Writing:* Writing can be a super-effective way of kickstarting your day. When you journal all your thoughts and emotions every day after waking up, it allows you to relieve yourself from all the mental clutter, unlocks your creative side, and sharpens your focus.

- *Working Out:* Working out is a great morning ritual that you can follow every day. When you work out daily, it helps you burn more fat, improves your blood circulation, and boosts your energy level. If you are interested in fitness and health, this is the perfect morning ritual for you. You can do some cardio exercises, or some strength training, or both. Depending on your suitability, create a workout routine for yourself and make sure to stick to that. If you don't stick to your routine, it won't be of much help.

-

2. Start Following the 80/20 Rule

The 80/20 rule states that almost 20% of the tasks you perform are responsible for yielding 80% of the results. It is why you should invest more time in tasks that can give you more significant results instead of wasting your time on tasks that yield little to no results. In this way, you can not only save time but also maximize your productivity. Most importantly, when you see the results after performing those tasks, you will be more motivated to complete the following tasks. After you have finished performing these tasks, now you can quickly move your concentration and focus towards other activities that you need to do throughout your day.

3. Practice Lots of Reading

Reading is a great habit and a great way to stimulate your creativity and gaining more knowledge. When you get immersed in reading, it calms you and improves your focus, almost similar to meditating. If you practice reading before going to bed, you are going to have a fantastic sleep. You can read non-fiction books, which will help you seek motivation, develop new ideas, and broaden your horizon. You can also get a lot of advice about how to handle certain situations in life.

4. Start Single-tasking

Multitasking is hard, and almost 2% of the world's total population can do this properly. You can try multitasking occasionally. If you keep on trying to do this all the time, it will form a mental clutter, and as a result, your brain won't be able to filter out unnecessary information. Many studies have suggested that it can severely damage your cognitive control and lower your efficiency when you multitask a lot. It is the main reason why you should try to do single-tasking more than multitasking. Prepare a list of all the tasks you need to perform in a day and start with the most important one. Make sure not to rush and to complete one thing at a time.

5. Start Appreciating More

Appreciating things is totally dependent on your mentality. For example, some people can whine and complain about a glass being half empty, whereas some people appreciate that there is half a glass of water. It totally depends on your point of view and way of thinking. People get blinded by the urge to reach success so much that they actually forget to appreciate the little things in life. If you are working and earning a handsome salary, don't just sit and complain about why you are not earning more, what you need to do to achieve that, etc. You should obviously aim high, but not at the cost of your well-being. When you practice gratitude, it increases your creativity, improves your physical health, and reduces your stress. You can start writing about the things you are grateful for in your journal every day before going to bed, make some time for appreciating your loved ones, or remind yourself of all the things you are grateful for before going to bed every day. If you are not happy with your current situation, you will not be happy in the future. You need to be happy and satisfied at first, and then only you can work on progressing further.

6. Always Keep Positive People Around You

When you have toxic people around you, it gets tough for you to stay in a good mood or achieve something good in life. Toxic people always find a way to pull you down and make you feel bad about yourself. You should always surround yourself with people who are encouraging and positive. When you do that, your life is going to be full of positivity.

7. Exercise on a Regular Basis

Start exercising regularly to maintain good health and enhancing your creativity and cognitive skills. It also increases your endurance level and boosts your energy. When you exercise regularly, your body produces more endorphins. These hormones work as anti-depressants.

8. Start Listening More

Effective communication is very important in maintaining both professional and personal relationships. For communicating effectively, you need to work on your listening capability first. You need to pay attention to the things said by others instead of focusing only on what you have to say. Listening to others will allow you to understand them better. When you listen to someone, it makes them understand that they are valued and that you are here to listen to them. When they feel important and valued, they also start paying attention to what you say, thereby contributing to effective communication. Don't try to show fake concentration while you are busy thinking about something else. When you listen more, you learn more.

9. Take a Break from Social Media (Social Media Detox)

Many studies have shown that excessive use of social media can contribute to depression. Most importantly, it wastes a lot of time because people meaninglessly scroll, swipe, and click for hours. It is a very unhealthy habit and is very bad for bothe physical and mental health. Sometimes you need to completely stop using social media for a while to reduce mental clutter and stress. Turn off your laptops and phones every day for a few hours. It will help you to reconnect with the surrounding world and will uplift your mood.

10. Start Investing More in Self-care

Make some time for yourself out of your busy schedule. It is going to boost your self-esteem, improve your mental health, and uplift your mood. You need to do at least one thing for yourself every day that will make you feel pampered and happy. You can prepare a mouth-watering meal, take a comfortable bubble bath, learn something new, or just relax while listening to music.

The moment you start introducing these habits in your daily, you will instantly see change. Remember that even a tiny step towards a positive change can give outstanding results if you stay consistent.

Chapter 4:
How to Learn Faster

Remember the saying, "You are never too old to learn something new"? Believe me, it's not true in any way you understood it.

The most reliable time to learn something new was the time when you were growing up. That was the time when your brain was in its most hyperactive state and could absorb anything you had thrown at it.

You can still learn, but you would have to change your approach to learning.

You won't learn everything, because you don't like everything going on around you. You naturally have an ego to please. So what can you do to boost your learning? Let's simplify the process. When you decide to learn something, take a moment and ask yourself this; "Will this thing make my life better? Will this fulfill my dreams? Will I benefit from it?".

If you can answer all these questions in a positive, you will pounce on the thing and you won't find anyone more motivated than you.

Learning is your brain's capability to process things constructively. If you pick up a career, you won't find it hard to flourish if you are genuinely interested in that particular skill.

Whether it be sports, singing, entrepreneurship, cooking, writing, or anything you want to pursue. Just ask yourself, can you use it to increase your creativity, your passion, your satisfaction. If you can, you will start learning it as if you knew it all along.

Your next step to learning faster would be to improve and excel at what you already have. How can you do that? It's simple yet again!

Ask yourself another question, that; "Why must I do this? Why do I need this?" if you get to answer that, you will find the fastest and effective way to the top yourself without any coaching. Why will this happen on its own? Because now you have found a purpose for your craft and the destination is clear as the bright sun in the sky.

The last but the most important thing to have a head start on your journey of learning is the simplest of them all, but the hardest to opt for. The most important step is to start working towards things.

The flow of learning is from Head to Heart to Hands. You have thought of the things you want to do in your brain. Then you asked your heart if it satisfied you. Now it's time to put your hands to work.

You never learn until you get the chance to experience the world yourself. When you go through a certain event, your brain starts to process the outcomes that could have been, and your heart tells you to give it one more try. Here is the deciding moment. If you listen to your heart right away, you will get on a path of learning that you have never seen before.

What remains now is your will to do what you have decided. And when you get going, you will find the most useful resources immediately. Use your instincts and capitalize your time. Capture every chance with sheer will and belief as if this is your final moment for your dreams to come true.

It doesn't matter if you are not the ace in the pack, it doesn't matter if you are not in your peak physical shape, it doesn't matter if you don't have the money yet. You will someday get all those things only if you had the right skills and the right moment.

For all you know, this moment right now is the most worth it moment. So don't go fishing in other tanks when you have your own aquarium. That aquarium is your body, mind, and soul. All you need is to dive deep with sheer determination and the stars are your limit.

Chapter 5:
How Getting Out of Your Comfort Zone Could Be The Best Thing Ever

A comfort zone is best described as the place where you feel comfortable and your abilities are not being tested, or a place where you don't have to try anything new or different. We have all heard the advice of getting out of our comfort zone. Its sure sounds like an easy phrase, but any advice is easier to give than to take. While it is true that the ability to take risks by stepping outside your comfort zone is the primary way by which we grow, it's also true that we are often afraid to take that first step. Embracing new experiences can bloom your life and could even change the direction of your career. Comfort zones are not really about comfort; and they are about fear. So, break the chains and step out; you will enjoy the process of taking risks and growing. Here are some ways to get out of your comfort zone to experience a better life.

1. Become Aware Of What's Outside The Comfort Zone

You believe so many things are worth doing, but the thought of disappointment and failure always holds you back. Identify the things that you are afraid of doing and assess the discomforts associated with them. Start working on them slowly and gradually. You will see how much progress you will make and how much you will grow following that. Once your discomforts no longer scare you, you will see how confident you will become in trying new things.

2. Have A Clear Sight About What You Have To Overcome

There would be many situations that get you anxious and uncomfortable. Please make a list of all of them and go deeper. The primary emotion associated with all of our negative thoughts that we try to overcome is fear. Are you afraid of public speaking because you are insecure about your voice? Do you get nervous around people and avoid talking to them for fear of being ignored? Be specific in your areas of discomfort, and then work on your insecurities to get more confident.

3. Get Comfortable With Discomfort

Expand your comfort zone to get out of it. Make it your goal to stop running away from the discomforts. If you can't make eye contact while talking, try locking it a bit more rather than immediately looking out. If you stay long enough and practice it, it will start to become less uncomfortable.

4. See Failure As A Teacher

Many of us are so scared of failures that we would prioritize doing absolutely nothing other than taking a shot at our dreams and goals. We have to treat our failures as a teacher. We learn more from failures than we do from successes. Take that experience that has caused you to fail and evaluate how you can take that lesson your next time so that the chance of success increases. Many of the world's famous people, and even billionaires and millionaires, failed the thousandth time before succeeding.

5. Take Baby Steps

Don't try to achieve everything at once. If you jump outside your comfort zone, the chances are that you will become overwhelmed and jump right back in. Always start by taking small steps, overcome the fear of little things first. It's the small steps along the journey that ensures our extraordinary destination. If you are afraid of public speaking, start by speaking to a smaller group of people or even your family and friends. This will help you built self-confidence, and you will be ready to talk on public platforms in no time.

6. Hang out with risk-takers:

If you want to become better at something, start hanging out with people who already took the risk, who already are doing the things you planned to do. Start emulating them. No one can give you the best insight into the situations than those who already have experienced it. Almost inevitably, their influence will start affecting your behavior, and you too will get a clear mind about things.

7. Be Honest With Yourself

Stop making excuses for the things that you are too afraid to do. You might be tricking your brain into thinking that maybe you don't have enough time to do your tasks. But in reality, you are scared of giving it a chance and risking failure. Don't make excuses but instead, be honest. You will be in a better place to confront what is truly bothering you, and this will increase your chance of moving forward.

8. Identify New Opportunities

Staying in your comfort zone is like sitting in a closed room or wearing blinders. You will convince yourself that you already dislike the things you didn't even try yet and only care about the already part of your life. But you have to put your walls down, not thickens them, and take risks. You will be amazed at how many opportunities you will be exposed to when you finally let yourself out.

Conclusion

It will seem scary at first to get out of your comfort zone, but it will be the best experience of your life. Don't jump right out of it; slowly push yourself past your comfort zone. You will eventually feel more and more comfortable about the new stuff you were too afraid to try.

Chapter 6:

7 Habits To Change Your Life

Consistently, habit drives you to do what you do—regardless of whether it's a matter of considerations or conduct that happens naturally. Whatever that is, imagine a scenario where you could saddle the power of your habits to improve things. Envision a day to day existence where you have a habit for finishing projects, eating admirably, staying in contact with loved ones, and working to your fullest potential. At the point when you have an establishment of beneficial routines, you're setting yourself up for a full, sound, and effective life.

Here are 7 habits that Can change your entire life.

1. Pinpoint and Focus Entirely on Your Key stone Routine.

Charles Duhigg, in his power book stipulates the essence of recognizing your Keystone Habit—the habit you distinguish as the main thing you can change about your life. To discover what that is for you, ask yourself, what continually worries you? Is it something you would that you like to stop, or something you would do and prefer not to begin? The cornerstone habit is distinctive for everybody, and it might take a couple of meetings of profound thought to pinpoint precisely what that habit is. Whichever propensity you're chipping away at, pick each in turn. More than each in turn will be overpowering and will improve your probability of neglecting to improve any habits. Be that as it may, don't really accept that you can just change one thing about yourself; it's really the inverse. Dealing with this one Keystone Habit can have a positive gradually expanding influence into the remainder of your life also.

2. Recognize Your Present Daily Practice and the Reward You Get From It.

Suppose you need to fabricate a habit for getting to the workplace a half hour early every day. You need to do this since you figured the extra peaceful time in the morning hours will assist you with being more gainful, and that profitability will be compensated by an expanded feeling of occupation fulfilment, and a generally speaking better workplace. As of now, you get to the workplace simply on schedule. Your present routine is to take off from your home in a hurry, at the specific time you've determined that (without traffic or episode) will get you to chip away at time. Your award is investing some additional energy at your home in the first part of the day, spending an additional half hour dozing or "charging your batteries" for the day ahead.

3. Take the Challenges Into Consideration.

Challenges are regularly prompts that push you to fall once more into old habits. In the case of having to get to work earlier, your challenges may lie in your rest designs the prior night, or in organizing plans with a partner. These difficulties won't mysteriously vanish so you need to consider them. In any case, don't let the presence of challenges, or stress that new difficulties will come up later on, discourage you from setting up your new propensities. In the event that your difficulties incorporate planning with others, make them a piece of your new daily practice, as I'll clarify later. At this moment, basically recognize what the difficulties or obstructions are.

4. Plan and Identifying Your New Routine.

Old habits never vanish; they are basically supplanted with new propensities. In the case of getting to the workplace earlier, the new standard includes going out a half hour sooner. On the off chance that the old habit was remunerated with the possibility that you'll have more energy for the day by remaining in your home longer, the new propensity needs to centre around the possibility that more rest doesn't really mean more energy. All in all, you'll need to address what you think you'll be surrendering by supplanting the old habit.

5. Reinforce a 30 Days Challenge.

By and large, your inability to minister beneficial routines basically comes from not adhering to them. A lot of studies show that habits, when performed day by day, can turn out to be important for your daily schedule in just 21 days. So set a beginning date and dispatch your game plan for a preliminary 30-day time span.

6. Empower Your Energy Through Setbacks

Here and there, it's not simply self-control that runs out. Now and then you are influenced from your ways by life "hindering" new objectives. In the event that something influences you from your test, the best game-plan is to assess the circumstance and perceive how you can get around, finished, or through that deterrent. Notwithstanding, when another propensity is set up, it really turns into our default setting. Assuming your standard habits are sound, unpleasant occasions are less inclined to lose you from your typical schedules. All in all, we're similarly prone to default to solid habits as we are to self-undermining habits, if those sound habits have become a piece of our ordinary daily practice.

7. Account Yourself and for Your Actions Publicly (Hold Yourself Accountable)

Your encouraging people are the most significant asset you will have at any point. Regardless of whether it's your closest companion, your accomplice or your Facebook posts, being responsible to somebody other than yourself will help you adhere to your objective. Simply remember that "responsible" isn't equivalent to "declaration". Anybody can advise the world they will rise ahead of schedule from here on out. However, on the off chance that that individual has a group of allies behind them, whom they routinely update, they are bound to stay with their new propensity during times when they are building up their new habit and inspiration is coming up short.

Chapter 7:
Creating successful habits.

Successful people have successful habits. If you're stuck in life, feeling like you're not going anywhere, take a hard look at your habits. Success is built from our small daily habits accumulated together, Without these building blocks, you will not get far in life. Precise time management, attention to detail, these are the traits of all who have made it big.

To change your life, you must literally change your life, the physical actions and the mindset.

Just as with success, the same goes with health.
Do you have the habit of a healthy diet and regular athletic exercises?
Healthy people have healthy habits.
If you are unhappy about your weight and figure, point the finger at your habits once again.

To become healthy, happy and wealthy, we must first become that person in the mind.
Success is all psychological.
Success has nothing to do with circumstances.
Until we have mastered the habits of our thinking we cannot project this success on the world.

We must first decide clearly who we want to be.

We must decide what our values are.

We must decide what we want to achieve.

Then we must discipline ourselves to take control of our destiny.

Once we know who we are and what we want to do,

Behaving as if it were reality becomes easy.

We must start acting the part.

That is the measure of true faith.

We must act as if we have already succeeded.

As the old saying goes: "fake it UNTIL YOU MAKE IT"

Commit yourself with unwavering faith.

Commit yourself with careful and calculated action.

You will learn the rest along the way

Every habit works towards your success or failure,

No matter how big or how small.

The more you change your approach as you fail, the better your odds become.

Your future life will be the result of your actions today.

It will be positive or negative depending on your actions now.

You will attain free-will over your thoughts and actions.

Success Comes From You

The more you take control, the happier you will be.

Guard your mind from negativity.
Your mind is your sanctuary.
Ignore the scaremongering.
Treat your mind to pure motivation.

We cannot avoid problems.
Problems are a part of life.
Take control of the situation when it arises.
Have a habit of responding with action rather than fear.

Make a habit of noticing everybody and respecting everybody.
Build positive relationships and discover new ideas.
Be strong and courageous, yet gentle and reasonable.
These are the habits of successful leaders.

Be meticulous.
Be precise.
Be focused.

Make your bed in the morning.
Follow the path of drill sergeants in the royal marines and US navy seals.
Simple yet effective,
This one habit will shift your mindset first thing as you greet the new day.

Success Comes From You

Choose to meditate.

Find a comfortable place to get in touch with your inner-self.

Make it a habit to give yourself clarity of the mind and spirit.

Visualize your goals and make them a reality in your mind.

Choose to work in a state of flow.

Be full immersed in your work rather than be distracted.

To be productive we need to have an incredible habit of staying focused.

It will pay off.

It will pay dividends.

The results will be phenomenal.

Every single thing you choose to make a habit will add up.

No matter how big or how small,

Choose wisely.

Choose the habit of treating others with respect.

Treat the cleaner the same as you would with investors and directors.

Treat the poor the same as you would with the CEO of a multi-national company.

Our habits and attitude towards ourselves and others makes up our character.

Choose a habit of co-operation over competition,

After all the only true competition is with ourselves.

It doesn't matter whether someone is doing better than us as long as we are getting better.

If someone is doing better we should learn from them.

Make it a habit of putting ourselves into someone else's shoes.

We might stand to learn a thing or two.

No habit is too big or too small.

To be happy and successful we must do our best in them all.

Chapter 8:
7 Ways To Discover Your Strengths

It is a fact that everybody has at least one skill, one talent, and one gift that is unique to them only. Everyone has their own set of strengths and weaknesses. Helen Keller was blind but her talent of speaking moved the world. Stephen Hawking theorised the genesis by sitting paralyzed in a wheelchair. The barber who does your hair must have a gifted hand for setting YOUR hair at reasonable prices—otherwise you wouldn't be visiting them.

See, the thing is, everyone is a prodigy at one thing or another. It's only waiting to be discovered and harnessed. Keeping that fact in mind…

Here are 7 Ways You can Discover Your Potential Strengths and Change Your Life Forever:

1. Try Doing Things That You Have Never Done

Imagine what would have happened if Elvis Presley never tried singing, if Michael Jordan never tried playing basketball or if Mark Zuckerberg never tried coding. These individuals would have been completely different persons, serving different purposes in life. Even the whole world would've been different today if some specific people didn't try doing some specific things in their lives.

Unfortunately, many of us never get to know what we are truly good at only because we don't choose to do new things. We don't feel the need to try and explore things that we have never done before in our lives. As a result, our gifted talents remain undiscovered and many of us die with it. So while the time is high, do as many different things you can and see what suits you naturally. That is how you can discover your talent and afterwards, it's only a matter of time before you put it to good use and see your life change dramatically.

2. Don't Get Too Comfortable With Your Current State

It is often the case that we cling on to our current state of being and feel absolutely comfortable in doing so. In some cases, people may even embrace the job that they don't like doing only because 'it pays enough'. And honestly, I totally respect their point of view, it's up to people what makes them happy. But if you ask me how one can discover their hidden talents—how one might distinguish oneself—then I'm going to have to say that never get used to doing one particular thing. If one job or activity occupies you so much that you can't even think of something else, then you can never go out to venture about doing new stuff. The key is to get out, or should I say 'break out' from what you are doing right now and move on to the next thing. What is the next thing you might want to try doing before you die? Life is short, you don't want to go on your whole life, never having experienced something out of your comfort bubble.

3. What Is The Easiest Thing You Can Do?

Have you ever found yourself in a place where you did something for the first time and immediately you stood out from the others? If yes, then chances are, that thing might be one of your natural strengths.

If you've seen 'Forrest Gump', you should remember the scene where Forrest plays table-tennis for the first time in a hospital and he's just perfect at the game. "For some reason, ping-pong came very naturally to me, so I started playing it all the time. I played ping-pong even when I didn't have anyone to play ping-pong with.", says Forrest in the movie.

So bottomline, pay attention to it if something comes about being 'too easy' for you. Who knows, you might be the world's best at it.

4. Take Self-Assessment Tests

There are countless, free self-assessment tests that are available online in all different kinds of formats. Just google it and take as many tests you like. Some of these are just plain and general aptitude tests or IQ tests, personality tests etc. while there are others which are more particular and tell you what type of job is suited for you, what kind of skills you might have, what you might be good at, and those kinds of things. These tests are nothing but a number of carefully scripted questions which reveal a certain result based on how you answered each question. A typical quiz wouldn't take more than 30 minutes while there are some short and long quizzes which might take 15 minutes and 45 minutes respectively.

Though the results are not very accurate, it can do a pretty good job at giving you a comprehensive, shallow idea of who you are and what you can be good at.

5. Make Notes On How You Deal With Your Problems

Everyone faces difficult situations and overcomes them in one way or the other. That's just life. You have problems, you deal with them, you move on and repeat.

But trouble comes in all shapes and sizes and with that, you are forced to explore your problem-solving skills—you change your strategies and tactics—and while at it, sometimes you do things that are extraordinary for you, without even realizing it. John Pemberton was trying out a way to solve his headache problem using Coca leaves and Kola nuts, but incidentally he made the world's coke-drink without even knowing about it. Lesson to be learned, see how YOU deal with certain problems and why is it different from the others who are trying to solve the same problem as you.

6. Ask Your Closest Friends and Family

People who spend a lot of time with you, whether it be your friend, family or even a colleague gets to see you closely, how you work, how you behave, how you function overall. They know what kind of a person you are and at one point, they can see through you in a manner that you yourself never can. So, go ahead and talk to them, ask them what THEY think your strongest suit can be—listen to them, try doing what they think you might turn out to be really good at, Who knows?

7. Challenge Yourself

The growth of a human being directly corresponds to the amount of challenge a person faces from time to time. The more a person struggles, the more he or she grows—unlocks newer sets of skills and strengths. This is a lifelong process and there's no limit on how far you can go, how high your talents can accomplish.

Now, one might say, "what if I don't have to struggle too much? What if my life is going easy on me?". For them, I'd say "invite trouble". Because if you are eager to know about your skills and strengths (I assume you are since you're reading this), you must make yourself face difficulties and grow from those experiences. Each challenge you encounter and overcome redefines your total strength.

Final Thoughts

To sum it up, your life is in your hands, under your control. But life is short and you gotta move fast. Stop pursuing what you are not supposed to do and set out to find your natural talents RIGHT NOW. Once you get to know your strengths, you will have met your purpose in life.

PART 2

Chapter 1:
7 Habits That Are Good For You

The cognitive ability to distinguish what is good from what is bad for us is an invaluable skill. Cherry-picking nutritive habits in a world full of all manner of indecency comes handy especially if you want to stand out from the crowd.

Here are 7 habits that are good for you:

1. <u>Waking Up Early</u>

The early bird catches the worm. Early risers have the opportunity to pick the best for themselves before the rest of the world is awake. It is healthy and prudent to wake up early and start your day before most people do. You leverage on opening your business early before your competitors. Besides, the preparedness of early risers is unmatched even as the day progresses.

Waking up early is not a reserve for 'busy people' only. It is for everyone in this world of survival for the fittest. We all have 24 hours in one day. The difference comes from how we use our time. One may spend more than 8 hours sleeping and another will spend just 6 hours for the same. You cannot sleep as if you are competing with the dead and expect to make it in the land of the living.

Early risers are active people. They are as alert as chamois, prepared for any eventuality.

2. Associate With Successful People

Show me your friends and I will show you what kind of person you are. Success, like most things, is contagious. In his book *48 laws of power*, Robert Greene writes '*avoid the unhappy and unlucky.*' This is not discrimination. Association with the unhappy and unlucky will contaminate you with negative energy.

Associate with successful people and you will follow their example. You will emulate their saving culture, their investment behavior, and their aggressiveness in business. In the shadow of the successful, you will attract positivity and grow exponentially. Maintain knit relationships with the successful.

3. Be Teachable

A teachable spirit will take you places where your character will not. A teachable person is capable of receiving correction graciously without perceiving it as demeaning. Do not be afraid of getting things wrong. Instead, be worried when you lack the humility to accept correction.

Being teachable is one of the greatest strengths you can have. We all are a work in progress, never finished products. What happens when you refuse to be under the tutelage of the successful and experienced? The greatest lessons are not learned in a classroom but the school of life.

4. Accepting Challenges

When challenged by circumstances we face, be the bigger brother/sister. Take challenges positively and work towards a solution instead of whining about this or that. Our patience, skills, and competence are sometimes put to the test. A test so subtle that we fail without even realizing it. When you have a positive mindset of accepting challenges, you will ace the game. Prove your worth wherever you are through your actions, never by your words.

When you accept a challenge and conquer it, it takes you to another level. The beauty of life lies in progress with the assurance that change is a constant. Accept challenges towards positivity and not the dark ones. Ignore that which derails your purpose or goes against your principles.

5. Learn When To Retreat and To Advance

The art of knowing when to push or pull is important in life. On the battlefield, retreating and advancing by troops is a call their leader makes. He decides that for his team based on his training, the immediate situation, and his judgment. Retreating is not a sign of weakness; neither is advancing a sign of strength. Both are strategies to win a war.

It is okay to retreat from a cause you were pursuing or to adjust your plans. Just make it worth your while. When you resume, be stronger than before. Again, when you retreat, do not succumb to the ridicule of your enemies when they mistake it for weakness. The fear of what the opinion of others (non-entities) is should not make you afraid of retreating to strategize.

When you make up your mind to advance with a noble course, advance skillfully. Do not advance blindly or ignorant of what you intend to achieve. Train your focus on the target.

6. Ask for help.

We are mortals; facing deficiencies here and there. We do not always have the answer to everything. Ask for help from the knowledgeable ones when in a quagmire.

Asking for help is not a weakness. It is appreciating the strengths of others. It is also appreciating the diversity of the human race that we are not endowed with everything. The silent rule is that you should be careful whom you approach for help. Some ill-intentioned people will sink you deep into trouble.

Nevertheless, asking for help is perfectly normal and it is something you should try sometimes. When you ask for help from the experienced, you save yourself the trouble of making messy mistakes. Learn through others who trod down the same road. Their lessons are invaluable; you will avoid their mistakes.

7. <u>Develop hobbies.</u>

Hobbies are those things you engage in for fun. They are very important because you take a break from your daily hustles. In your hobbies, you are carefree. You do not have to worry about your boss or business partners.

Hobbies are meant to be fun. If you are not having fun when doing your hobbies, probably they are no longer one. You should consider finding new ones. All work without play makes Jack a dull boy.

Hobbies are good for you. Go for swimming or that road trip, find a sport and play for fun, go beyond singing in the shower, travel everywhere you desire, or even start watching that TV series you are always curious about. Variety is the spice of life. Do not be afraid to spice up your life with all that your heart desires.

The above 7 habits are good for you. They will help you grow and increase your productivity in all you do.

Chapter 2:
10 Habits That Make You More Attractive

Being attractive does not necessarily connote physical appearance. More than the physical appearance, attraction renders the mental, emotional, and spiritual energy irresistible to others. Some people radiate with their energy and confidence regardless of whether they have money, looks, or are socially connected. These people are just irresistible, and you will find that people will always approach them for advice, help, or even long-term companionships. What makes them more attractive? Their sense of self-worth is always from within their souls as contrasted with how they look from outside. They don't seek validation from others- but find it within themselves.

However, this is not genetically connected, but a habit that we can build within ourselves. You need to pursue and maintain such habits for the benefit of a greater you.

Here are 10 habits that make you more attractive:

1. Connect With People More Deeply.

Attractive people are always likable people, and being likable is a skill. Being likable means that you should be interested in hearing others out rather than spending all the time thinking and talking about yourself. As entrepreneur Jim Rohn puts it- "Irresistible or likeable people possess an authentic personality that enables them to concentrate more on those around them." This requires that you are in most cases over yourself, meaning that you don't spend more time only thinking about yourself.
To have this habit going on in you, try to take conversations seriously. Put that phone down and listen! Learn what those around you are into - Ask questions, enquire about their dreams, fears, preferences, and views on life. Focus on what is being said rather than what the response is or what impact that might have on you. Always aim to make others everyone feel valued and important.

2. Treat Everyone With Respect.

Being polite and unfailingly respectful is the key to being likable. If you are always rude to others, you will find that over time people will tend to avoid you. You should strive to not only be respectful to someone you know and like, but also to strangers that you come across with. Attractive people treat everyone with the same respect they deserve bearing in mind that no one is better.

3. Follow the Platinum Rule.

The commonly known version of the golden rule is that you should treat others the same way you want them to treat you. This comes with a major flaw: the assumption that everyone aspires to be treated similarly. The rule ignores the fact people are different and are motivated differently. For instance, one person's love for public attention is another's person's execrate. However, you can opt for this flaw by adopting the platinum rule instead. The notion is that you should only treat others as they want to be treated. Attractive people are good at reading others and quickly adjust to their style and behavior, and as a result, they can treat them in a way that makes them feel comfortable.

4. Don't Try Too Hard To Put an Impression.

Attractive people who are easily likable don't try too hard to impress. Liking someone comes naturally, and it depends on their personality. Hence if you spend most of the time bragging about your success or smartness, you are simply harming yourself without knowing it. People who try too hard to be liked are not likable at all. Instead they come across as narcissistic and arrogant. If you wish to be an attractive person choose to be humble and down-to-earth instead. People will see your worth with their own two eyes.

5. **Forgive and Learn From Your Mistakes.**

Learning from our mistakes is synonymous with self-improvement. It is proven that psychological traits are essential in human mating or relationships, meaning that both intelligence and kindness are key. Being intelligent, in this case, doesn't necessarily mean the PHDs or Degrees. It means that a person can demonstrate intelligence by learning from mistakes they make and handling the same well. You demonstrate this also by being kind to yourself whenever you make a mistake and avoiding the same mistake in the future. Attractive people know how to not take themselves too seriously and to have a laugh at themselves once in a while.

6. **Smile Often**

People tend to bond unconsciously with the body language portrayed while conversing. If you are geared towards making people more attracted to you, smile at them when conversing or talking to them. A smile makes other people feel comfortable in conversations, and in turn, they do the same to you. The feeling is remarkably good!

7. Likable People Are Authentic and Are Persons of Integrity.

People are highly attractive to realness. Attractive people portray who they are. Nobody has to expend energy or brainpower guessing their objective or predicting what they'll do next. They do this because they understand that no one likes a fake. People will gravitate toward you if you are genuine because it is easy to rely on you. On the flip side, it is also easy to resist getting close to someone if you don't know who they really are or how they actually feel.

People with high integrity are desirable because they walk their talk. Integrity is a straightforward idea, but it isn't easy to put into action. To show honesty every day, attractive people follow through with this trait. They refrain from gossiping about others and they do the right thing even if it hurts them to do so.

8. Recognize and Differentiate Facts and Opinions.

Attractive people can deal gracefully and equally with divisive subjects and touchy issues. They don't shy away from expressing their views, but they clarify that they are just that: opinions, not facts. So, whenever you in a heated discussion, be it on politics or other areas with your peers, it is important to understand that people are different and are just as intelligent as you are. Everyone holds a different opinion; while facts always remain facts. Do not confuse the two to be the same.

9. Take Great Pleasure in The Little Things

Choose joy and gratitude in every moment – No matter if you are feeling sad, fearful, or happy. People who appreciates life for its up and downs will always appear attractive to others. Choose to see life as amazing and carefully approach it with joy and gratitude – Spread positive vibes and attract others to you that are also positive in nature. View obstacles as temporary, not inescapable. Everyone has problems, but it is how you deal with it each day that is important here. Optimistic people will always come out on top.

10. Treating friendships with priority.

True friendships are a treasure. When you take your time and energy to nourish true friendships, you will naturally develop others skills necessary to sustain all forms of relationships in your life. People will always gravitate to a person who is genuinely friendly and caring. They want to be a part of this person's life because it brings them support and joy. Take these friendships with you to the distance.

Bonus Tip: Do Your Best to Look Good.

There is a huge difference between presentation and vanity. An attractive person will always make efforts to look presentable to others. This is comparable to tidying up the house before you receive visitors - which is a sign of gratitude to others. Don't show up sloppily to meetups and parties; this will give others the impression that you don't care about how you look which may put off others from approaching you. Always try your best in every situation.

Conclusion: Bringing it all in

Attractive people don't get these habits simply floating over their beds. They have mastered those attractive characteristics and behaviors consciously or subconsciously - which anyone can easily adopt.

You have to think about other people more than you think about yourself, and you have to make others feel liked, appreciated, understood, and seen. Note, the more you concentrate on others, the more attractive you will appear and become without even trying.

Chapter 3:
10 Habits That Damage Your Brain

Our brain is the most vital and unrivaled organ in the body. I am talking about the 100 billion-plus brain cells that are responsible for controlling everything that our body does. But, what I find odd is that often, we tend to neglect our brain health over other parts of our body. We work out and are constantly taking care of our body yet we forget about the most important organ that is basically keeping us alive! Most people are seemingly unaware that our brain requires training and exercise too. I bet most of you already know how crucial habits are in shaping you and your life but did you know that some habits even kill your brain cells? What if I told you that you could be damaging your own brain? Yes. You heard me right. We engage in certain habits in our day-to-day lives that are seemingly harmless but have are damaging our brains. Some of these damages that our brain suffers are known to be long-term and even fatal in some cases. Some examples of brain damage are Dementia and Alzheimer's.

If you want to know what these habits are that you might be engaging in, I am going to discuss ten such habits that are damaging your brain without even you noticing that you should immediately remove them from your life.

1. **Skipping Breakfast**

How frequently do you skip breakfast? Well, most people skip breakfast due to an ongoing diet, to save time, some do not feel hungry in the morning or just because they do not think it is important enough. However, did you know that skipping breakfast actually leads to brain damage? Remember that our body has gone without any food for approximately 8 hours. When we sleep, our body uses the stored-up nutrients. So, therefore, you should always remember to replenish these nutrients so that the brain and the body have enough energy to function properly throughout the day. Similarly, another Japanese study of 80,000 subjects conducted in a period of over 15 years showed that people who skipped breakfast frequently suffered from a stroke and low blood pressure, which is very harmful to the brain. Did you know that not having breakfast lowers the blood glucose level of the brain? So, the next time you decide to pass on your breakfast, think about the damage you are causing to your own brain.

2. Consuming Too Much Sugar

How often do you crave for and indulge in candies and sugary drinks? Well, because another reason that leads to brain damage is when you consume too much sugar. I bet you already know how eating too much sweet stuff can affect your body health drastically, giving you diabetes and obesity. You might be planning to cut off your sugar intake to have that perfect waistline, but another very important reason why you might want to do so is to protect your brain from being undeveloped. Yes, too much sugar hinders your brain's capacity to develop. It is because when you consume a lot of candies and sweets, it disrupts your body's ability to absorb the important nutrients and proteins, which then results in your body not being able to send these to your brain. This makes your brain malnutritioned and stops its development.

3. Smoking

Smoking is probably the most harmful habit that a person might have. All of us already know smoking gives us a ton of diseases related to the heart and lungs, and not to forget cancer. Well, another reason why you should quit smoking starting today is that it brings about a ton of brain-related illnesses too. Did you know that smoking damages your brain membrane and neural viability of your brain that is responsible for balance, coordination, and motor skills? Not only that, smoking thins the cortex of your brain that deals with language, memory, and perception. Smoking is also a major cause of Dementia, Alzheimer's, and even death. It also leads to inflammation of the brain resulting in illnesses such as Multiple Sclerosis. Considering all this information, I would suggest you take quitting smoking more seriously.

4. Not Getting Enough Sleep

Did you know that sleep is crucial for both our physical and mental health? So, do you sleep enough? Or too much? The number of hours that you sleep has a direct impact on the functioning of your brain. Sleep deprivation is one of the most common things of this generation. But do you know that it can cause your brain to shrink its size? It can lead to serious issues such as depression, extreme daytime drowsiness, impaired memory. Studies have shown that it is only during the deep sleep cycle that the toxins in your brain are released. Even one night of sleep deprivations leads to issues such as not being able to recall new information and dysfunctioning of your brain. You are basically killing your brain cells by not improving your sleeping habits that will result in memory loss.

5. Covering Your Head When Sleeping

What if I told you that the way you sleep is also known to cause brain damage? You might be wondering how. But if you are among the many that cover their heads while they sleep, you are causing your brain damage. This is because it leads to carbon dioxide buildup as you will be intaking more carbon dioxide than oxygen to your brain. This can even cause you to have Dementia at an early age.

6. Blasting Music on Your Headphone

While listening to music on your headphones may be convenient, did you know that listening to loud music and not giving your ears a break causes you brain damage? If you are one of those who constantly listen to music, then you should probably give it a little more thought because you are damaging not only your ears but also your brain. Medical experts say that this can lead to hearing problems and also memory loss. Hearing problems are mostly related to brain problems such as loss of brain tissue. So, it is time you adjust your volume and gives your ears a break so that you can preserve your hearing and protect your brain from further damage.

7. Not Drinking Enough Water

Do you have a habit of over-looking your water intake? Because let me tell you that your brain needs an adequate amount of water to function properly, think faster, and focus better. It is no news that our body made up of 70% of water, right? Therefore, water is crucial to the body and the brain. Researchers say that dehydration has immediate effects on the brain. Even 2 hours of a heavy task without proper hydration can lead to disruptive cognitive functions. The brain needs sufficient water to clean out the toxins in our brains and so that it can carry the nutrients and proteins from our body to the brain. So, don't forget to drink enough water starting today!

8. No Exercise

Did you know that exercising not only improves your body but greatly helps in improving the functioning of your brain? So, how frequently do you exercise? You do not necessarily have to follow a rigorous routine or join a gym. It could be a swim in the pool from time to time or a jog in the morning. Exercising increases your heart rate, which then helps pump more oxygen to the brain. With the release of happy hormones known as endorphins, exercising also helps you remain younger. Not only that, but exercising is also known to produce and release other hormones that help the brain to grow and develop.

9. Overeating

Overeating is when you eat more than what your body needs. Eating too much is never a good idea as we all know the terrible consequences it brings about, such as an increase in weight, obesity, and cholesterol, among others. But among all this, did you know that overeating affects your brain too? It makes the arteries of your brains harder, leading to a decrease in mental power. Not only that, it creates an unhealthy cycle of overeating out of boredom, it also disrupts your sleeping habits, all of which cause stress and thus decrease your brain health more.

10. Working When Sick

Do not forget that your brain works the hardest, and so it is vital that you give it a rest. You can never get your brain back to its shape no matter how much you rest after you have overused it. Therefore, whenever you are sick, like having a headache or flu, or even when you are exhausted, do not push your brain to work. This will lead to a decrease in the effectiveness of the brain. If you have a habit of working like this, you are making your brain suffer severe and irreversible damage.

That brings us to the end of the ten habits that damage our brain. If you identified and related to one or more of these habits, then it is time that you remove them completely from your life so that you can preserve your most important body part - the brain, which also means protecting your whole body.

Chapter 4:
8 Steps To Develop Beliefs That Will Drive you To Success

'Success' is a broad term. There is no universal definition of success, it varies from person to person considering their overall circumstances. We can all more or less agree that confidence plays a key role in it, and confidence comes from belief.

Even our most minute decisions and choices in life are a result of believing in some specific outcome that we have not observed yet.

However, merely believing in an ultimate success will not bring fortune knocking at your door. But, it certainly can get you started—take tiny steps that might lead you towards your goal. Now, since we agree that having faith can move you towards success, let's look at some ways to rewire your brain into adopting productive beliefs.

Here are 8 Steps to Develop Beliefs That Will Drive You To Success:

1. **Come Up With A Goal**

Before you start, you need to decide what you want to achieve first. Keep in mind that you don't have to come up with something very specific right away because your expectations and decisions might change over time. Just outline a crude sense of what 'Achievement' and 'Success' mean to you in the present moment.

Begin here. Begin now. Work towards getting there.

2. **Put Your Imagination Into Top Gear**

"Logic will take you from A to B. Imagination will take you everywhere", said Albert Einstein.

Imagination is really important in any scenario whatsoever. It is what makes us humans different from animals. It is what gives us a reason to move forward—it gives us hope. And from that hope, we develop the will to do things we have never done before.

After going through the first step of determining your goal, you must now imagine yourself being successful in the near future. You have to literally picture yourself in the future, enjoying your essence of fulfilment as vividly as you can. This way, your ultimate success will appear a lot closer and realistic.

3. Write Notes To Yourself

Writing down your thoughts on paper is an effective way to get those thoughts stuck in your head for a long time. This is why children are encouraged to write down what is written in the books instead of memorizing them just by reading. You have to write short, simple, motivating notes to yourself that will encourage you to take actions towards your success. It doesn't matter whether you write in a notebook, or on your phone or wherever—just write it. On top of that, occasionally read what you've written and thus, you will remain charged with motivation at all times.

4. Make Reading A Habit

There are countless books written by successful people just so that they can share the struggle and experience behind their greatest achievements. In such an abundance of manuscripts, you may easily find books that portray narratives similar to your life and circumstances. Get reading and expand your knowledge. You'll get never-thought-before ideas that will guide you through your path to success. Reading such books will tremendously strengthen your faith in yourself, and in your success. Read what other successful people believed in—what drove them. You might even find newer beliefs to hold on to. No wonder why books are called 'Man's best friend'.

5. Talk To People Who Motivates You

Before taking this step, you have to be very careful about who you talk to. Basically, you have to speak out your goals and ambitions in life to someone who will be extremely supportive of you. Just talk to them about what you want, share your beliefs and they will motivate you from time to time towards success. They will act as powerful reminders. Being social beings, no human can ever reject the gist of motivation coming from another human being—especially when that is someone whom you can rely on comfortably. Humans have been the sole supporter of each other since eternity.

6. Make A Mantra

Self-affirming one-liners like 'I can do it', 'Nothing can stop me', 'Success is mine' etc. will establish a sense of firm confidence in your subconscious mind. Experts have been speculative about the power of our subconscious mind for long. The extent of what it can do is still beyond our grasp. But nonetheless, reciting subtle mantras isn't a difficult task. Do it a couple of times every day and it will remain in your mind for ages, without you giving any conscious thought to it. Such subconscious affirmations may light you up in the right moment and show you the path to success when you least expect it.

7. Reward Yourself From Time To Time

Sometimes, your goals might be too far-fetched and as a result, you'll find it harder to believe in something so improbable right now. In a situation like this, what you can do is make short term objectives that ultimately lead to your main goal and for each of those objectives achieved, treat yourself with a reward of any sort—absolutely anything that pleases you. This way, your far cry success will become more apparent to you in the present time. Instant rewards like these will also keep you motivated and make you long for more. This will drive you to believe that you are getting there, you are getting closer and closer to success.

8. Having Faith In Yourself

Your faith is in your hands alone. How strongly you believe in what you deserve will motivate you. It will steer the way for self-confidence to fulfill your inner self. You may be extremely good at something but due to the lack of faith in your own capabilities, you never attempted it—how will you ever know that you were good at that? Your faith in yourself and your destined success will materialize before you through these rewards that you reserve for yourself. You absolutely deserve this!

Final Thoughts

That self-confidence and belief and yourself, in your capabilities and strengths will make you work towards your goal. Keep in mind that whatever you believe in is what you live for. At the end of the day, each of us believed in something that made us thrive, made us work and move forward. Some believed in the military, some believed in maths, some believed in thievery—everyone had a belief which gave them a purpose—the purpose of materializing their belief in this world. How strongly you hold onto your belief will decide how successful you will become.

Chapter 5:
7 Habits of Healthy Relationships

Relationships are the social strings that hold us together. We are tied to our loved ones by relationships. Sadly, we also regret being linked, by our relationships, to people of questionable character. There are those relationships we are in by default and others by design – meaning we are in them in our free will, without any coercion whatsoever.

Here are 7 habits of healthy relationships:

1. <u>Making It Symbiotic</u>

It is a selfish foundation but it is what relationships truly are. Healthy relationships are symbiotic between the partners. Both parties benefit from its existence. They are equal partners and bring something to the table.

When partners in a relationship have a mutual interest in a course, they will work towards achieving it. They understand that any failure is a loss to all of them. This is a powerful drive to make them work towards staying united because they need each other.

Symbiosis is the mechanism of adaptation to nature. The relationship between bees and flowers is an example of a healthy relationship. The bees depend on nectar from flowers to make food while flowers depend on bees to be agents of cross-pollination. It is a win-win for both of them.

2. <u>Pursuing A Common Goal</u>

Two heads are better than one. When people are united by a course they believe in, the relationship is stronger and healthier. There is a reason more than their selfish interests that brings them together.

The promise of success by achieving this common goal makes the relationship healthy – devoid of any backstabbing from either party. As long as partners in a relationship have a common objective, nothing can come between them.

If you have a relationship you want to salvage, find a common ground to stand on. This will give you more reason not to give up on the relationship. Consider the relationship between a man and his fiancé. What is common between them is love and the desire to start a family together. Challenges will come their way but whatever holds them together is greater than what divides them. In the end, love wins.

3. <u>They Are Not Exclusive</u>

Some relationships, especially romantic ones, tend to be exclusive to two people. The two people give themselves to each other completely, withholding nothing. Any foreign person that comes between them is considered hostile and unwanted.

However, healthy relationships are not exclusive. They give room to the third voice of reason which will whisper some advice or rebuke some ills they do. The view of a third eye is golden. It will see what the two of you overlook. The simple, repetitive, toxic habits that bring down relationships will not thrive in yours because you have allowed an experienced eye to be the guardian angel.

This is not to imply that there should be no privacy. Privacy is beautiful in relationships. It only stops being one when it overrides your well-being and stops your relationship from budding.

4. It Happens Naturally

Murphy's law states that *anything that can go wrong will go wrong*. Relationships are not exceptional either. Regardless of how many times you try to resuscitate a dying relationship, if it can go wrong then it will go wrong.

Healthy relationships are those that happen automatically. There is no within or external force that works on making them stick. There is a special vibe from those in the relationship. They bond naturally. Partners in automatic relationships do not struggle to be together, it is as if nature herself has blessed them 'to be fruitful and multiply.'

In automatic relationships, you do not ignore the red flags. This kind is not blind. When you see red flags in your relationships and continue living in denial, murphy's law will apply. Settle down to re-evaluate; is it that your spouse is too perfect, or are you ignoring the red alerts all over?

5. Balanced Selfishness

What a vice for healthy relationships to thrive in! They are selfish enough to put their interests above those of everyone else. Do not judge; it is completely natural in this world of survival for the fittest. Most importantly is that those in relationships act as a unit. They are not selfish to each other but to the rest of the world.

This vice waters the success of relationships. Not everyone has your best interests at heart. Some will try to infiltrate your relationship and cause havoc. Beware of such people. It is the reason why relationships must be selfish.

Consider the example of bees. They jealously and viciously guard their queen and the honey they make. They are selfish with it and their safety is non-negotiable. Even bee farmers have to wear protective clothing when they want to harvest honey. Their selfishness is what unites them, how beautiful!

6. <u>Making Investments</u>

Investment is a sign of trust. You invest in someone or something you have confidence in. Partners in healthy relationships invest in each other because they trust in each other. The best foundation of healthy relationships is trust because in it, you can be yourself.

Why should you be in a relationship with someone you cannot trust? The fact that you cannot be yourself with your partner is sufficient not to be involved with them.

You invest in relationships because you are assured of returns. The safest place to be is in a fulfilling one. Healthy relationships go far because their partners invest their time and resources in them.

7. <u>Clearly Marked Boundaries</u>

Regions and territories are demarcated by boundaries. They partition countries, provinces, and estates. So important are they that border disputes are treated with utmost seriousness anywhere in the world. The latest border dispute in East Africa being the unresolved maritime dispute between Kenya and Somalia.

Likewise, healthy relationships have boundaries. The partners are mature enough not to suffocate each other. It is paramount that in a relationship, for example, between a man and his fiancée, that they allow each other space to live their lives.

Healthy relationships are not suffocating or dominating. There is a boundary that those in relationships do not cross. If not for anything else, it is for peace to prevail. It does not mean that trust is lacking in the relationship. On the contrary, it signals that you trust your partner enough not to betray whatever relationship you share.

These 7 habits are paramount for healthy relationships. When you religiously observe them, you will have a testimony of a turning point in your relationships.

Chapter 6:

Stay Focused.

A razor sharp focus is required to bridge the gap
between our vision and our current circumstances.
Stay focused on the vision we want,
despite the current reality.
It's challenging to believe you will be rich when you are poor,
healthy if you are sick,
but it is necessary to achieve that vision.

Focus on the desired result.
Focus on the next step towards that goal.
Without focus on these elements there can be no success.
Stay focused on the positive elements,
solutions over problems.

The expected reward over the fear, loss and pain along the way.
What we focus on will become.
Therefore we have to maintain our eyes on the prize.

Be results driven.
Always focus on bringing that result closer.
Focus on what your grateful for.
Gratefulness brings more of that into your life.
Focus on problems on the other hand brings more problems.

If we focus on a big goal today,
we might not be ready yet,
but we will become ready on the way.

Commit to the necessary changes you know you need.
Get ourselves ready for that goal.
So many never act simply because they don't know how.
They don't feel ready.

Success Comes From You

We can achieve nearly anything if we focus on it.

Think carefully about what you focus on.
It is critical to both your success and failure.
Know exactly what you want.
See the odds of a successful happy life increase by unfathomable amounts.

How can we be happy and successful if we never define what that is?
It's not about what you are, or what you were in the past.
It is all about what you are becoming and want to become.

We cannot let circumstances or the world decide that.
We must use our free will and decide who and what we will become and focus fully on that.
Wishing, succumbing to the days whim, will never bring lasting success.
Success requires serious commitment and focus on that outcome.
Exude a fanatical level of focus.
Be exuberated in the pursuit of success.

The most successful often focus on work for over 100 hours per week.
They give up most social interaction and even sleep to make that dream happen.
They do not find this hard or stressful because they are pursuing something they enjoy.

Focus on something you enjoy.
Stop spending your time and energy on a job that you hate.
Work in an area you enjoy.
It makes focusing and achieving success easier.

Keep in mind that your time is limited.
Is what you're doing right now moving you towards your goal?
If not stop.

It is crucial that you enjoy your journey.
Start planning some leisure time into your days.
The goal is to remain balanced while you stick to your schedule.

Success Comes From You

If you focus on nothing, you will receive nothing.
If you do nothing, you will become nothing.

Your focus is everything.
Get specific with your focus to steer your ships in the direction of the solid fertile land you desire.
Aim higher as you focus on bigger and better things.

Why focus on plan b if you believe in plan a?
Why not give all your focus to that?

Stay focused on the best result regardless of the perceived situation.
The world is pliable.
It will mould and change around you based on your thoughts and what you focus on.
Your free will means you are free to focus on what you want and ignore what you don't.

Focus on a future of greatness.
A future where you are healthy, happy, and wealthy.
See the limits as imaginary and watch them break down before you.
Understand that you are powerful and what you think matters in your life.

Become who you want to be,
Not who others think you should be.
This shift is one of the quickest roads to happiness.

When you focus on what you love,
You draw more of it into our lives.
You will become happier.

You must focus on a future that makes you and your family happy.
You must stay steadfast with an unwavering faith and focus on that result.
Because with faith and focus anything is possible.

Chapter 7:
Six Steps To Create A Vision For Your Life

Hi everyone, for today's video, we are going to talk about how to create life's visions. You might be thinking, "why do we need to make these visions?" or "what are these visions for?".

Let me ask you this question, have you ever felt so stuck in where you are? That feeling when you wanna move and be somewhere else because you don't like where you are but you don't know where to go either? That is the worst feeling ever, right?

Creating a vision for your life will save you from being stuck and lost. These visions are the pictures you create about the life that you want to live.

Here are 6 Steps To Start Envisioning Your Future

Step number 1, identify what matters to you. Ask yourself, "what's really important to me?". Is it health? Career? Wealth? Relationships? Passion? Time? It could be a balance of all those things. What legacy would you want to leave in this world? Identifying what truly matters to you and what you really value gives you a destination of where you want to be. Having these in mind, all your plans and decisions will be centered towards your destination.

Next step is thinking ahead, but at the same time, also believing that it is already happening for you right now. Be specific in chasing what you want, don't just simply limit yourself to what you think is socially acceptable. If you limit your choices to what seems to be reasonable, you are disconnecting yourself from your true potentialDon't compromise.. Be as audacious as you want to be, it's your own life anyway! You have all the right to dream as big as you want. Talk as if your dreams are happening right now. When you have this big dream, you won't settle for less just because it is what's available at the moment.

Step number 3, assess and challenge your motives. Ask yourself, "is this the kind of life I wanna live because it is what the society is expecting from me?", "am I doing this because this is what everybody else is doing?" Knowing your real motive towards your visions will help you uncover what your heart really desires. You might even be surprised by what you'll discover within you when you remove all the layers that the world has planted in you.

Next step, be sure that your visions are aligned with a purpose. You don't need to know exactly what your life purpose is, unless you've already figured that out somehow. But your visions should be relevant to how you want your life to be. For example, if your goal is to maintain your mental well-being, your vision might be to live your life peacefully while focusing on the things that truly matter. Your vision should serve you the purpose into making your life as pleasing as you want it.

Step number 5 is to be accountable for your own visions. Don't tie your visions into someone else's hands. Your visions may involve direct impact to others but make sure that your visions are not dependent on other people. Why? Because people, just like the seasons, change. People come and go. The version of the people in your life right now is not how they will be for the rest of their lives. And so are you. Hold these visions in your own hands and make sure you execute it diligently and faithfully.

Last step is to make room for changes. You will grow as a person, that is a fact. You won't have the same exact priorities all through your life. And that's okay. Whatever you want to change into is valid. Your goals and dreams are all valid. Changes are inevitable so don't be afraid if you have to change what's working for you from time to time.

While you are in the process of making your life's visions, be as creative as you can. Although the world is not a wish-granting factory, remember that through your hard work and perseverance, nothing is really impossible. You have everything in you to achieve your goals and live through your visions. You just need to be clear about what you really want or where you wanna be.

Remember that our days in this world are limited. We won't be able to live our lives to the fullest if we are just merely existing or living by default. We are humans. And as humans, we have the power to lead the life we truly desire. Sometimes, we are just one decision away from it.

I hope what we've talked about today will not just inspire you to make your life's visions but also help you to understand why you need to make them. You deserve a kind of life that will excite you to wake up everyday because you know what you are waking up for.

Chapter 8:
How To Succeed In Life

"You can't climb the ladder of success with your hands in your pocket."

Every day that you're living, make a habit of making the most out of it. Make a habit of winning today. Don't dwell on the past, don't worry about the future. You just have to make sure that you're winning today. Move a little forward every day; take a little step every day. And when you're giving your fruitful efforts, you're making sure you're achieving your day, then you start to built confidence within yourselves. Confidence is when you close your eyes at night and see a vision, a dream, a goal, and you believe that you're going to achieve it. When you're doing things, when you're productive the whole day, then that long journey will become short in a matter of time.

Make yourself a power list for each day. Take a sheet of paper, write Monday on top of it and then write five critical, productive, actionable tasks that you're going to do that day. After doing the task, cross it off. Repeat the process every day of every week of every month till you get closer to achieving your goals, your dreams. It doesn't matter if you're doing the same tasks every day or how minor or major they are; what matters is that it's creating momentum in things that you've believed you couldn't do. And as soon as the momentum gets completed, you start to believe that you can do something. You eventually stop writing your tasks down because now they've become your new habits. You need a reminder for them. You don't need to cross them off because you're going to do them. The power list helps you win the day. You're stepping out of your comfort zone, doing something that looks uncomfortable for starters, but while doing this, even for a year, you will see yourself standing five years from where you're standing today.

Decide, commit, act, succeed, repeat. If you want to be an inspiration to others, a motivator to others, impact others somehow, you have to self-evaluate certain perceptions and think that'll help you change the way you see yourself and the world. Perseverance, hard-working, and consistency would be the keywords if one were to achieve success in life. You just have to keep yourself focused on your ultimate goal. You will fall a hundred times. There's always stumbling on the way. But if you have the skill, the power, the instinct to get yourself back up every time you fall, and to dig yourself out of the whole, then no one can stop you. You have to control the situation, Don't ever let the situation control you. You're living life exactly as it should be. If you don't like what you're living in, then consider changing the aspects. The person you are right now versus the person you want to be in the future, there's only a fine line between the two that you have to come face-to-face with.

Your creativity is at most powerful the moment you open your eyes and start your day. That's when you get the opportunity to steer your emotions and thoughts in the direction that you want them to go, not the other way around. Every failure is a step closer to success. We won't succeed on the first try, and we will never have it perfect by trying it only once. But we can master the art of not giving up. We dare to take risks. If we never fail, we never get the chance of getting something we never had. We can never taste the fruits of success without falling. The difference between successful people and those who aren't successful is the point of giving up.

Success isn't about perfection. Instead, it's about getting out of bed each day, clearing the dust off you, and thinking like a champion, a winner, going on about your day, being productive, and making the most out of it. Remember that the mind controls your body; your body doesn't hold your mind. You have to make yourself mentally tough to overcome the fears and challenges that come in the way of your goals. As soon as you get up in the morning, start thinking about anything or anyone that you're grateful for. Your focus should be on making yourself feel good and confident enough to get yourself through the day.

The negative emotions that we experience, like pain or rejection, or frustration, cannot always make our lives miserable. Instead, we can consider them as our most incredible friends that'll drive us to success. When people succeed, they tend to party. When they fail, they tend to ponder. And the pondering helps us get the most victories in our lives. You're here, into another day, still breathing fine, that means you got another chance, to better yourself, to be able to right your wrongs.

Everyone has a more significant potential than the roles they put themselves in.

Trust yourself always. Trust your instinct—no matter what or how anyone thinks. You're perfectly capable of doing things your way. Even if they go wrong, you always learn something from them. Don't ever listen to the naysayers. You've probably heard a million times that you can't do this and you can't do that, or it's never even been done before. So what? So what if no one has ever done it before. That's more of the reason for you to do it since you'll become the first person to do it. Change that 'You can't' into 'Yes, I definitely can.' Muhammad Ali, one of the greatest boxers to walk on the face of this planet, was once asked, 'how many sit-ups do you do?' to which he replied, 'I don't count my sit-ups. I only start counting when it starts hurting. When I feel pain, that's when I start counting because that's when it really counts.' So we get a wonderful lesson to work tirelessly and shamelessly if we were to achieve our dreams. Dr. Arnold Schwarzenegger beautifully summed up life's successes in 6 simple rules; Trust yourself, Break some rules, Don't be afraid to fail, Ignore the naysayers, Work like hell, And give something back.

Chapter 9:
Becoming High Achievers

By becoming high achievers we become high off life, what better feeling is there than aiming for something you thought was unrealistic and then actually hitting that goal.

What better feeling is there than declaring we will do something against the perceived odds and then actually doing it.

To be a high achiever you must be a believer,

You must believe in yourself and believe that dream is possible for you.

It doesn't matter what anyone else thinks , as long as you believe,

To be a high achiever we must hunger to achieve.

To be an action taker.

Moving forward no matter what.

High achievers do not quit.

Keeping that vision in their minds eye until it becomes reality, no matter what.

Your biggest dream is protected by fear , loss and pain.

We must conquer all 3 of these impostors to walk through the door.

Not many do , most are still fighting fear and if they lose the battle, they quit.

Loss and pain are part of life.

Losses are hard on all of us.

Whether we lose possessions, whether we lose friends, whether we lose our jobs, or whether we lose family members.

Losing doesn't mean you have lost.

Losses are may be a tough pill to swallow, but they are essential because we cannot truly succeed until we fail.

We can't have the perfect relationship if we stay in a toxic one, and we can't have the life we desire until we make room by letting go of the old.

The 3 imposters that cause us so much terror are actually the first signs of our success.

So walk through fear in courage , look at loss as an eventual gain, and know that the pain is part of the game and without it you would be weak.

Becoming a high achiever requires a single minded focus on your goal, full commitment and an unnatural amount of persistence and work.

We must define what high achievement means to us individually, set the bar high and accept nothing less.

The achievement should not be money as money is not our currency but a tool.

The real currency is time and your result is the time you get to experience the world's places and products , so the result should always be that.

The holiday home , the fast car and the lifestyle of being healthy and wealthy, those are merely motivations to work towards. Like Carrots on a stick.

High achievement is individual to all of us, it means different things to each of us,

But if we are going to go for it we might as well go all out for the life we want, should we not?

I don't think we beat the odds of 1 in 400 trillion to be born, just to settle for mediocrity, did we?

Being a high achiever is in your DNA , if you can beat the odds , you can beat anything.

It is all about self-belief and confidence, we must have the confidence to take the action required and often the risk.

Risk is difficult for people and it's a difficult tight rope to walk. The line between risk and recklessness is razor thin.

Taking risks feels unnatural, not surprisingly as we all grew up in a health and safety bubble with all advice pointing towards safe and secure ways.

But the reward is often in the risk and sometimes a leap of blind faith is required. This is what stops most of us - the fear of the unknown.

The truth is the path to success is foggy and we can only ever see one step ahead , we have to imagine the result and know it's somewhere down this foggy path and keep moving forward with our new life in mind.

Success Comes From You

Know that we can make it but be aware that along the path we will be met by fear , loss and pain and the bigger our goal the bigger these monsters will be.

The top achievers financially are fanatical about their work and often work 100+ hours per week.
Some often work day and night until a project is successful.
Being a high achiever requires giving more than what is expected, standing out for the high standard of your work because being known as number 1 in your field will pay you abundantly.
Being an innovator, thinking outside the box for better practices, creating superior products to your competition because quality is more rewarding than quantity.
Maximizing the quality of your products and services to give assurance to your customers that your company is the number 1 choice.
What can we do differently to bring a better result to the table and a better experience for our customers?
We must think about questions like that because change is inevitable and without thinking like that we get left behind, but if we keep asking that, we can successfully ride the wave of change straight to the beach of our desired results.
The route to your success is by making people happy because none of us can do anything alone, we must earn the money and to earn it we must make either our employers or employees and customers happy.

To engage in self-promotion and positive interaction with those around us, we must be polite and positive with everyone, even with our competition.
Because really the only competition is ourselves and that is all we should focus on.

Self-mastery, how can I do better than yesterday?
What can I do different today that will improve my circumstances for tomorrow.
Little changes add up to a big one.
The belief and persistence towards your desired results should be 100%, I will carry on until... is the right attitude.
We must declare to ourselves that we will do this , we don't yet know how but we know that we will.
Because high achievers like yourselves know that to make it you must endure and persist untill you win.
High achievers have an unnatural grit and thick skin , often doing what others won't, putting in the extra hours when others don't.
After you endure loss and conquer pain , the sky is the limit, and high achievers never settle until they are finished.

PART 3

Chapter 1:
How To Stop Wasting Time

In the inspiring words of Marcia Wider, "It's how we spend our time here, and now, that really matters. If you are fed up with the way you have come to interact with time, change it."

Indeed, time waits for no man. The ticking of the clock should be a startling revelation to you that how precious our time on this earth is. A study conducted at the University of Calgary shows that the ratio of chronic procrastination has increased from 5% in 1978 to 26% in 2007. In other words, you don't need more time. You have to do MORE with the time you already have. Stop wasting your time on the things that don't really matter. Do you realize how many seconds and minutes and hours do we waste every day on stuff that doesn't even let us come close to reaching our goals? If you've ever come to ask yourself, "where does the time go?" then maybe you should re-think how and on what you're spending your time.

"A man who dares to waste one hour has not discovered the value of time." Charles Darwin. There are only as many as 24 hours in a day, and you've got to make sure that each of them counts for something. There's a date on the left side of the tombstone, that's the date on which you were born. When you die, another date is engraved on the right side of your tombstone, but that dash, that line that you see in the middle of both these dates, decides how much you left your mark on other people's lives as well as your own, how much you were able to impact others, that dash represents how you lived your life in the timeframe that you were given.

We all get the same amount of time. A homeless person or a beggar that wanders here and there all day brings the same amount of time as the most successful businessman. It's what we do with that time, how we presume the ticking of the clock that genuinely matters. Life flickers by us in the blink of an eye. And what do we do about that? We only give excuses and justifications. "I don't have time to go to the gym, and maybe I'll start tomorrow. I'll start studying tomorrow; one day of taking a break won't make a difference" NO! It would make all the difference in the world. Stop fearing and pitying yourself and get up. Stop wasting your time because it's a depreciating asset, and you won't get any of it back.

You have to take the first step. You can't just live your life fearing the challenges and efforts you have to put in to get somewhere higher in life. Procrastinating, watching your favorite TV show adds up to so much time, even for an hour each day. And that time is nothing but wasted. Imagine the knowledge you can gain in that one hour of each day, imagine the work that you could do, the language that you can learn, the instrument that you can learn to play. So start investing your time into something productive rather than just lying here making defenses.

"Newton's first law of productivity" states that objects at rest tend to stay at rest until they're acted upon. That book on your shelf isn't going to read itself, those weights in the gym aren't going to move by themselves, that long due essay isn't going to write itself, YOU. HAVE. TO. DO. IT! And you have to do it now. Don't wait for another hour or another day or another week; you have to take that leap of faith; you have to take that risk. Specify your days, prioritize your to-do list, eliminate all the distractions. Nothing will make you happier than knowing that you're making progress towards becoming a better version of yourself. Take breaks, but get yourself back up to your goals. Don't waste your time! "Whatever you want to do, do it now! There are only so many tomorrow's." – Pope Paul VI.

FOCUS! You should be terrified of living a life on the sidelines. Of not achieving anything whether you're 6, 16, or 60. Of doing nothing and watching the time passes by, of not making any progress and not being able to come closer to your dreams, your goals. Stop being stagnant! Start working towards your passion, your dreams, your aspirations. The separator between the people that win and lose is what we do with that time, with those seconds that we get in a day. Start working towards self-mastery, and you will begin to see the difference in all the dimensions of your life. So concentrate on developing yourself because if you don't, I guarantee you that you will make a settlement, and most people have, and most of us already have. The proper function of a man is to live, not just only to exist. We shall not waste our days trying to prolong them only, but we shall use our time effectively.

Time is free, but it's also priceless. It's perhaps the most essential commodity in this world. Once you've lost it, you can never get it back. Look back and see how many hours and days and years have you wasted doing absolutely nothing? Don't shy up from the tough things. We can't make excuses and then expect to be successful at the same time. We have to get up every day and make sure we don't quit ourselves, our goals, our dreams, our passions. Make mistakes, make them thousand times over, but make sure you learn something from every single one of them. We can't travel back to time and change the past. So don't dwell on the things that happened yesterday or months ago. Start working towards your future. We only have a limited time here on earth. It's better to spend time waiting for the opportunity to take action than miss the chance.

"Determine never to be idle. No person will have occasion to complain of the want of time who never loses any. It is wonderful how much can be done if we are always doing." - Thomas Jefferson.

Chapter 2:
How To Share Your Talent

Hi everybody! I hope everyone is doing well. Today, we're going to talk about sharing your talent to the world. As humans, it is so natural to us to feel that we want to share a part of ourselves to the world around us through one way or another. We have this yearning to create or produce something that will benefit other people. We feel a sense of fulfillment in knowing that we did something to positively impact other people's lives. And one way to do this is by sharing our talents.

So, let's get to the steps on how you'll be able to share your talents.

First, you have to discover your talent. Know what you can offer. Believe that you have something in you that you can offer to the world to be the light that it needs and find it. Listen to your intuition and subconscious mind. Most of the time, your intuition knows what you have and how you'll be able to let it out. Know that everyone is unique and the world needs your authenticity and whatever that you can give. Don't allow society or cultural norms to dictate what you should be doing or where you should be good at.

Next, practice what you believe you're good at. Discovering your talents doesn't always mean that you'll be instantly great at it. You still need to make efforts to hone them. Take your time to practice and focus on your progress. Even the most talented musicians or athletes that ever walk this on planet spent so much time practicing and improving their crafts. So, don't give up if you feel like you are not going anywhere with your talent.

Third step is to be open to all possibilities. Sometimes, we want to be really good at one thing and we end up not giving ourselves a chance to be open to other opportunities. Life is full of surprises. Don't limit yourself in one field because you won't know what are the other things you're good at if you'll be so afraid to try something new. You're probably pursuing to hone your talent in music but you might also be good in writing. You won't know that you write really well if you don't give yourself a chance to try it. So, be open to all the possibilities and don't ever hold back.

Next step is to find your tribe. Your tribe is the people that share the same visions as you. They are the ones that believe in you and support you in your endeavors as you hone your talents. They make you feel that you and your talents are valued. And you do all these to them too. You support one another. Being with the right people that empower you to realize your full potential is an important part of your journey. So, if you'll ever find your tribe, stay with them and you'll surely go places.

Fifth step is to get yourself out in the world. Don't hesitate to show yourself and what you can offer. Remember that there's only one you in the whole world and that is your power. Even if some people will reject you and your work, there will always be people that you will inspire by just merely showing up. Don't let every rejection stop you in sharing your talent. Many successful authors have faced multiple rejections before their works got published. A lot of great actors and actresses have experienced failed auditions before they get to perform in televisions and cinemas. Many engineers have received bad grades when they were students before they got their degree. But they all made it to where they are now because they did not let any of the rejections they received to stop them in honing their talents and pursuing their dreams. So, don't give up on your talents. With perseverance and hardwork, you will also shine and light someone's world.

When you share your talent, you're not only making a positive impact on other people's lives but it also improves your own being. There is no other more fulfilling feeling in the world than to know that you've made someone's day a little brighter by sharing a part of yourself. As humans, we only have one chance to walk on this planet. And if we could make this world a little better than how we find it, that one chance is totally worth it. Life is beautiful as they say. But it will be even better if we share it with others.

I hope today's video will move you to start sharing your talent. If you like this, give this a thumbs up and subscribe to my channel for more. I'll see you on the next one!

Chapter 3:

How to Reprogram Your Mind for Success

Your routines are the things that drive you through life. Your routines are driven by your emotions. Your emotions are a sum of your past. Your past is a sum of incidents. These incidents may be related to a person or a thing, which in turn make your life exciting.

You start your day with a thought. A thought that wakes you up every day. A unique thought that everyone experiences every morning. These thoughts are the driving force for you to get up whether you like it or not.

These thoughts may be fear-driven or love memories. So your brain creates emotions in your subconscious mind which in turn dictates your daily tasks and routine.

You might be having doubts about a leave from a job that you might deserve because you can't get the doubt of getting fired out of your mind.

You might be remembering a loved one that you want to see today.

You may be hoping to get some good news today.

So you have a set routine every day, that you follow without even ever pondering on day-to-day life. And this is the ultimate failure of your purpose in life.

A routine that is not getting you forward in life isn't worth living with. But you are not able to think about it because your mind and your subconscious have taken over your body.

As all these obvious things are being stated, close your eyes, put some music on, shut the doors or sit on a bench in a quiet part. Tell your mind to get rid of those memories that drive your emotions. Leave your body motionless and try to take deep breaths.

As you start doing this, you will feel an immediate thought kick in your subconscious. Your mind will be making you feel like something is missing or if you had something to do.

This is an uncomfortable state of mind. But now is your time to be your own master. Tell your subconscious that it is your will that leads you, but not the emotions and your mind.

Success Comes From You

You have to realize the reality and make it seem more acceptable to your brain. You have to make it feel confident and feel that it is helping you to stay commited in any situation that comes across in your life.

You need to become conscious in this hectic world of involuntary unconsciousness.

You have to make yourself ready for the unpredictable future. Because if you are not ready for the future, you are still drowning in your past.

Everyone's past is toxic. Even good memories can be toxic. One might ask how.

The memories of the past either make your stay in the bed or they make you hope full of chances to come with luck. But luck is rarely lucky.

You cannot be a free man till you dive out of your personal reality that your brain has created to keep you in your comfort zone. You cannot become successful if you stay on your laptop or your phone interacting with the world via social media and emails.

You have to create your own environment by making new friends, taking new jobs, asking questions to your partner, making a change in your natural habitat.

Your mind is the curator of your environment and the people in it. So you have to change your environment by making your mind commit to your orders.

Give your mind a free space to rehabilitate and renew itself. Give it a chance to imagine new things. Make it wander off like a herd of cattle in the grasslands. Let it flow without any emotion, just to create enough space for new realities to pop in. As soon as it does, you will find yourself in a new realm of happiness and success.

Chapter 4: How to Acknowledge The Unhappy Moments?

In today's video we will talk about how we can embrace the unhappiness moments in our lives and turn them into power and strength that will carry us through life gracefully.

We all have moments in life when we are not happy, we're scared, we're apprehensive, mildly depressed even, and the pain is difficult to endure. Whether it be because we have lost a friend, someone we love, or that we are simply not happy at our jobs. There could be a million reasons for our unhappiness.

In these trying times we only want an escape. To escape from our pain, our unhappy feelings because we are not ready to deal with the things that are going wrong in our lives. We don't want to acknowledge our unhappy moments because this makes us grieve and inflict more pain.

All these ways of avoiding the acknowledgment only perpetuate our feelings in long run. Avoidance only brings us misery and suffering in the long run. It keeps us from living to our fullest potential. It keeps us from the very fact that there is light at the end of the tunnel, and that we need to keep moving forward.

It is very important that you acknowledge your unhappy moments because you can only move forward with confidence once you accept that life being unhappy is simply a part of life. How can you admire happiness and the joys in your life if you have not gone through any unhappy moments? If you have nothing to compare it to?

It is not always easy to acknowledge the unhappy moments in life. But here are 5 powerful ways to help you along with the process.

Recognize the Reason of your unhappiness

First step of acknowledgment is to recognize the problem, find the real reason why you are unhappy. If, for example, you think you are not happy at your job, instead of pointing fingers at the obvious issues you are facing, ask yourself the deeper questions. Questions like, do I feel like I belong here? Do I feel I'm making a difference? Is what I am doing fulfilling my true desires? If the answer to those questions is a resounding no, it could be that your heart is, at that very moment, not in this job. You might be feeling as though you are spinning on a hamster wheel, going around in circles with nowhere in sight. It is very important to understand the true reason for your unhappiness because you cannot cut the stem and think that the tree will not grow again.

Take a moment and stop

Once you have found the problem, take a moment, and just stop right there. Don't suppress the feelings. Take a deep breath and sit with it for a while. Just sit there and be with it. Acknowledge that you have identified the essence of the unhappiness that had been festering in you for a while.

And be glad that you now have something to work with to change your situation.

Accept what it is

Once you have found the root of the problem it's time to accept it. As Thick Nhat mentioned in his book "Peace is every step". He writes that it is important to mentally acknowledge our feelings. Say out loud if you feel like it, "I can accept that I am experiencing intense unhappiness right now. And that it is okay. And that I will be okay."

Once you have embraced your moments of unhappiness you can overcome the feelings and move forward with peace.

If you are embracing your moments of unhappiness, you can create a mental space and see around it instead of being enmeshed in them. This space will open new doors and help you overcome your feelings as you embrace new beginnings that will soon come your way.

Plan Next Best Move

Now that you have successfully identified the reason for your unhappiness, it is time to find out what your next best move is. In life we never really know what the next right move is, we can only hope and trust that our decisions will work for us in the end.

Take the time to write down the things you want and the things that can change your situation. Things that can potentially move you out from a place of unhappiness. Going back to the previous problem that we have discussed, if it is your job that is causing distress in your life, what are the potential ways you can apply to mitigate the problem, would it be to quit or could you find a compromise somewhere. Talking to a colleague, a friend, or even your boss to let you explore your areas of creativity and things you excel at could be a welcome change.

Whatever the potential may be, no matter how big or small, you have the power to change your situation. Don't stay trapped in that situation for too long as it will only bring you down further along the road.

Believe Things Will Work Out In The End

Hope is a very powerful thing. Now that we have a plan, we need to have faith and just believe that our actions will pay off. We can never predict the future, and so taking one step at a time is the best thing we can do. We have to believe that whatever we are doing to change our situation will turn our unhappiness around sooner or later.

Final Thoughts

Happy and unhappy moments are part of life, like day and night, light, and darkness.

If you only believe in one thing, believe that change is the only constant and that bad times don't last forever. You will be happy again and you will move forward gracefully. And this is only possible if acknowledge your unhappy moments.

Happiness Is just right around the corner.

Chapter 5:

Five Steps to Clarify Your Goals

Today, we're going to talk about how and why you should start clarifying your goals.
But first, let me ask you, why do you think setting clear goals is important?

Well, imagine yourself running at a really fast speed, but you don't know where you're going. You just keep running and running towards any direction without a destination in mind. What do you think will happen next? You'll be exhausted. But will you feel fulfilled? Not really. Why? Because despite running at breakneck speed and being busy, you have failed to identify an end point. Without it, you won't know how far or near you are to where you are supposed to be. The same analogy applies to how we live our lives. No matter how productive you are or how fast your pacing is, at the end the race, if you don't have clear goals, you will simply end up wondering what the whole point of running was in the first place. You might end up in a place that you didn't intend to be. Neglecting the things that are most important on you, while focusing on all the wrong things- and that is not the best way to live your life.

So, how can we change that? How can we clarify our goals so that we are sure that we are running the race we intended to all along?

1. Imagine The Ideal Version of Yourself

Try to picture the kind of person you want to be. The things you want to have. The people you want around you. The kind of life that your ideal self is living. How does your ideal-self make small and big decisions? How does he or she perceive the world? Don't limit your imagination to what you think is pleasant and acceptable in society.

Fully integrate that ideal image of yourself into your subconscious mind and see yourself filling those shoes. That is the only way that you'll be able to see it as a real person.

Remember that the best version of yourself doesn't need to be perfect. But this is your future life so dream as big as you want, and genuinely believe that you'll be able to become that person someday in the near future.

2. Identify The Gap Between Your Ideal and Present Self

Take a hard look at your current situation now and ask yourself honesty: "How far am I away now from the person I know I need to become one day? What am I lacking at present that I am not doing or acting upon? Are there any areas that I can identify that I need to work on? Are there any new habits that I need to adopt to become that person?

Be unbiased in your self-assessment as that is the only way to give yourself a clear view of knowing exactly what you need to start working on today. Be brutally honest with your self-evaluation.

It is okay to be starting from scratch if that is where are at this point. Don't be afraid of the challenge, instead embrace and prepare yourself for the journey of a lifetime. It is way worse not knowing when and where to begin than starting from nothing at all.

3. Start Making Your Action Plan

Once you have successfully identified the gap between your present self and your ideal self, start to list down all the actions you need to take and the things that need to be done. Breakdown your action plan into milestones. Make it specific, measurable and realistic. If your action plans don't work the way you think they will, don't be afraid to make new plans. Remember that your failed plans are just part of the whole journey so enjoy every moment of it. Don't be hard on yourself while you're in the process. You're a human and not a machine. Don't forget to rest and recharge from time to time. You will be more inspired and will have more energy to go through your action plan if you are taking care of yourself at the same time.

4. Set A Timeline

Now that you have identified your overarching goal and objectives, set a period of time when you think it is reasonable for a certain milestone to be completed. You don't need to be so rigid with this timeline. Instead use it as sort of a guiding light. This guide is to serve as a reminder to provide a sense of urgency to work on your goals consistently. Don't beat yourself up unnecessarily if you do not meet your milestones as you have set up. Things change and problems do come up in our lives. As long as you keep going, you're perfectly fine. Remember that it is not about how slow or how fast you get to your destination, it is about how you persevere to continue your journey.

5. Aim For Progress, Not Perfection

You are living in an imperfect world with an imperfect system. Things will never be perfect but it doesn't mean that it will be less beautiful. While you're in the process of making new goals and working on them as you go along, always make room for mistakes and adjustments. You can plan as much as you want but life has its own way of doing things. When unforeseen events take place, don't be afraid to make changes and adjustments, or start over if you must. Even though things will not always go the way you want them to, you can still be in control of choosing how you'll move forward.

As humans, we never want to be stuck. We always want to be somewhere better. But sometimes, we get lost along the way. If we have a clear picture of where we want to be, no matter how many detours we encounter, we'll always find our way to get to our destination. And you know what, sometimes those detours are what we exactly need to keep going through our journey.

Chapter 6:
6 Habits of Oprah Winfrey

When anyone utters the name "Oprah Winfrey," one of her most iconic quotes comes to mind: "You get a car, and everyone else gets a car." While most business people applaud the "to-do roster," Oprah is not one of them; instead, she values meditation, no alarms, and limiting business operations to the necessary minimum. From a poor rural Mississippi upbringing to getting a full scholarship and to landing a seat on the morning talk program, Baltimore Is Talking, to now solidifying her reputation as a global legend and America's first black billionaire, with a net worth of US$2.5 billion, you might be wondering – exactly how she does it?

Oprah Winfrey maintains a series of daily routines-from getting up early to work out to practicing Gratitude. This daily routine, as she notes, keeps her happy, grounded, and humble.

Here are six daily habits from the legend herself that you might want to make your own.

1. **Her Day Starts With Morning Rituals.**

Oprah Winfrey starts her mornings with a sequence of spiritual exercises, allowing her body to wake up and her mind to focus on Gratitude and self-reflection. She meditates for approximately 20 minutes. If the weather is nice, she sits in her lawn chair with her eyes closed, simply reminiscing on the previous day and imagining her aspirations for the day ahead. She noted that starting the day slowly allows her mind to wake up and become entirely focused on the day ahead.

2. Working Out Every Morning.

Oprah's journey to weight loss has been a struggle over the years. She opened up on her efforts with maintaining a healthy weight and fitness program. She highlighted in an interview that she loves sweating it up through the regular old-fashioned cardio exercises, explicitly on an elliptical machine followed by a treadmill. She then follows with some regular bodyweight training before warming up for some sit-ups.

Although there is ongoing research on whether a better fitness routine should be in the morning or the evening, substantial studies describe several morning fitness benefits. To mention a few, You'll eat fewer calories; you'll have more energy throughout the day, burn more bothersome fat cells, and sleep better when the sun goes down.

3. She Consumes a Lot of Vegetables.

If you don't pay attention when your mother or your partner softly encourages you to eat more of Mother Earth's natural creations, maybe you'll listen to Oprah Winfrey.

Oprah confessed in an interview that she values her lunch more than any other meal, and one of her meals go-to involves a big, overflowing salad of green goodness. She noted that the salad is usually from the veggies from her home garden. As she put its's "as a rule, if we can grow it, we don't buy it."

You probably don't need us to tell you that veggies are excellent for your diet. Still, science backs up Winfrey's meal plan, as a well-balanced, vegetable patch diet can help fight cancer, heart disease, diabetes, and hypertension, among other conditions.

4. Oprah Schedules Time To Unwind.

There's no doubt that Winfrey's itinerary would be overwhelming for most people, with regular meetings, phone conversations, and traveling, but achieving this degree of esteem necessitates astute management and perseverance. However, if you look into the lives of individuals at the pinnacle of success, such as Winfrey, you'll notice that they constantly make time to unwind.

In an interview about her daily life, Winfrey stated that she relaxes before retiring to bed by reading frequently. Though you may not have Winfrey's gorgeous fireplace to warm you up as you flip the pages over, the research found that individuals who read before bed are less anxious than those who watch Netflix.

5. Practicing Gratitude daily.

The benefits of practicing Gratitude have been proven for centuries, even though gestures to the same have become popular recently. Oprah maintains with her volumes of gratitude diaries that she usually jots down before going to bed. She makes a list of things that have given her tremendous joy or which she is grateful for.

Implementing this habit will not only improve your health but also increase your empathy and self-confidence. One study suggests that thinking about what you're thankful for rather than contemplating on the to-do list each night helps better your sleep.

6. She Manages Her Finances.

You'd think someone of Winfrey's caliber would employ someone to manage her finances, but while she got a whole team, she oversees the minutiae of her fortune daily. She claims that she cannot delegate all financial decisions to others because she had a poor upbringing and prefers to understand what comes in and what goes out of her earnings. She noted during an interview that it is crucial for her to personally manage her finances as doing so relieves her from surprises of what she has and doesn't have.

While most of us struggle with the very thought about money, research has shown that the more you train yourself to handle your finances, the better your chances of becoming wealthy.

Conclusion

Just as Oprah, if you are invariably striving to achieve greatness in all life aspects, you must maintain a couple of healthy habits. If Oprah's journey inspires you, then flexing to the above routine might be your thing. Who knows!

Chapter 7:
6 Concerning Effects of Mood On Your Life

By definition, mood is the predominant state of our mind which clouds over all the other emotions and judgements. Our mood represents the surface-level condition of our emotional self.

Mood is very versatile and sensitive. Subtle changes in our surroundings or even changes in our thoughts directly affect mood. And consequently, our mood, being the leader of our mental state, affects us, as a whole—even impacting our life directly.

Take notes of these following points so that you can overpower your mood and take complete control of your life.

Here Are 6 Ways How Changes In Your Mood Can Impact Your Life:

1. Mood On Your Judgement and Decision-Making

Humans are the most rational beings—fitted with the most advanced neural organ, the brain. Scientists say that our brain is capable of making one thousand trillion logical operations per second and yet still, we humans are never surprised to make the stupidest of judgements in real life.

Well, along with such an enormous 'Logical reasoning' capacity, our brains also come with an emotional center and that is where mood comes in to crash all logic. Most of the decisions we make are emotional, not logical. Since our emotions are steered by mood, it is no surprise that we often make irrational decisions out of emotional impulses.

But again, there are also some instances where mood-dictated decisions reap better outcomes compared to a logical decision. That's just life.

2. Mood Affects Your Mental Health

While our mood is a holistic reflection of our mental state caused by various external and internal factors, it is also a fact that our mood can be the outcome of some harboring mental illness. Both high degree of euphoria and depression can be an indication of mood disorder—just on two opposite ends of the spectrum.

There is no specific cause behind it except that it is a culmination of prolonged mood irregularities. And mood irregularities may come from anywhere i.e. worrying, quarrelling, drug abuse, period/puberty, hormonal changes etc. If such mood irregularity persists untreated, it may deteriorate your overall mental health and result in more serious conditions. So, consider monitoring your mood changes often.

3. Correlation Between Mood and Physical Well-Being

We have heard the proverb that goes, "A healthy body is a healthy mind". Basically, our body and mind function together. So, if your body is in a healthy state, your mind will reflect it by functioning properly as well. If on the other hand your body is not in a healthy state, due to lack of proper nutrition, sleep, and exercise, then your mind will become weak as well. Yes, according to research, having a persistent bad mood can lead to chronic stress which gradually creates hormonal imbalance in your body and thus, diseases like diabetes, hypertension, stroke etc. may arise in your body. Negative moods can also make you go age faster than usual. So having a cheerful mood not only keeps you happy but also fuels your body and keeps you young. Aim to keep your body in tip top condition to nourish the mind as well.

4. Effect Of Your Mood On Others

This is obvious, right? You wouldn't smile back at your significant other after you have lost your wallet, spilled hot coffee all over yourself and missed the only bus to your job interview.

Your mood overshadows how you behave with others. The only way to break out of this would be to meditate and achieve control over your emotional volatility—believe that whatever happened, happened for a reason. Your sully mood doesn't warrant being hostile with others. Instead, talk to people who want the best of you. Express your griefs.

5. Mood As A Catalyst In Your Productivity

Tech giants like Google, Apple, Microsoft all have certain 'play areas' for the employees to go and play different games. It is there to remove mental stress of the employees because mood is an essential factor in determining your productivity at work-place. According to experts, people with a negative mood are 10% less productive in their work than those who are in a positive mood. This correlation between mood and productivity is an important thing to be concerned about.

6. Mood Change Your Perspective

Everyone has their own point of view. Perspectives of people vary from individual to individual and similarly, it varies depending on the mood of an individual. On a bad day, even your favorite Starbucks drink would feel tasteless. It doesn't mean that they made a bad drink—it means that you're not in the mood of enjoying its taste. So, how you perceive things and people is greatly affected by your mindset. Pro-tip: Don't throw judgement over someone or something carrying a bad mood. You'll regret it later and think "I totally misread this".

Final Thoughts

Our mood has plenty of implications on our life. Though our mood is an external representation of our overall mental state, it has its effect on very miniscule aspects of our life to large and macroscopic levels. In the long run, our mood alone can be held responsible for what we have done our whole life—the choices we've made. Though it is really difficult to control our mood, we can always try. Meditating may be one of the possible ways to have our mood on the noose. Because no matter what happens, you wouldn't want your whole life to be an outcome of your emotional impulses would you?

Chapter 8:
5 Ways To Adopt Right Attitude For Success

Being successful is a few elements that require hard work, dedication, and a positive attitude. It requires building your resilience and having a clear idea of your future ahead. Though it might be hard to decide your life forward, a reasonable manner is something that comes naturally to those who are willing to give their all. Adopting a new attitude doesn't always mean to change yourself in a way but, it has more meaning towards changing your mindset to an instinct. That is when you get stressed or overworked is because of an opposing point of view on life.

With success comes a great sense of dealing with things. You become more professional, and you feel the need to achieve more in every aspect. Don't be afraid to be power-hungry. But, it also doesn't mean to be unfair. Try to go for a little more than before, each step ahead. Make your hard work or talent count in every aspect. Make yourself a successful person in a positive manner, so you'll find yourself making the most of yourself. And don't give up on the things you need in life.

1. **Generate Pragmatic Impressions**

"The first impression is the last impression." It's true that once you've introduced yourself to the person in front of you, there is only a tiny chance that you'll get to introduce yourself again. So, choosing the correct wording while creating an impression is a must. You need to be optimistic about yourself and inform the other person about you in a way that influences them. An impression that leaves an effect on them, so they will willingly meet you again. A person must be kind and helpful towards its inferior and respectful towards their superior. This is one of the main characteristics for a person to be a successful man or woman. And with a negative attitude, the opposite occurs. People are more inclined to work without you. They nearly never consider you to work with them and try to contact you as little as possible. So, a good impression is significant.

2. Be True To Your Words

Choose your wording very carefully, because once said, it can't be taken back. Also, for a successful life, commitment is always an important rule. Be true to what you said to a person. Make them believe that they can trust you comfortably. So, it would be best if you chose your words. Don't commit if you can't perform. False commitment leads to loss of customers and leads to the loss of your impression as a successful worker. Always make sure that you fulfill your commands and promises to your clients and make them satisfied with your performance. It leads to a positive mindset and a dedication to work towards your goal.

3. A Positive Personal Life

Whatever you may be doing in your professional life can impact your personal life too. Creating the right mindset professionally also helps you to keep a positive attitude at home. It allows you to go forward with the proper consultation with your heart. It will make you happier. You'll desire to achieve more in life because you'll be satisfied with your success. It will push to go furthermore. It will drive you towards the passion for desiring more. Hard work and determination will continue to be your support, and you will be content will your heart. By keeping a good attitude, you'll be helping yourself more than helping others.

4. Be Aggressive and Determined

Becoming goal-oriented is one of the main factors evolving success in your life. If you are not determined to do your work, you'll just accept things the way others present you. It will leave you in misery and deeply dissatisfied with yourself. Similarly, you'll tend to do something more your way if you are goal-oriented and not how others want. You'll want to shale everything according to your need, and you become delighted with yourself and the result of your hard work. Always keep a clear view of your next step as it will form you in to your true self. Don't just go with the flow, but try to change it according to your wants and needs.

5. Create Your Master Plan

Indeed, we can't achieve great things with only hard work. We will always need to add a factor or to in our business. But by imagining or strategizing, some plans might be helpful. With hard work and some solid projects, we will get our desired outcome. If not, at least we get something close. And if you chose the wrong option, then the amount of hard work won't matter. You'll never get what you want no matter the hard work. So, always make sure to make plans strategically.

Conclusion

By keeping a positive attitude, you'll not only be helpful to others but to yourself too. Make sure you keep the proper manner—a manner required to be a successful person. Do lots of achievements and try to prove yourself as much as possible. Try keeping a good impact on people around you in everything you do. Have the spirit and courage to achieve great heights. And be sure to make moat of yourself. Consistency is the key.

Chapter 9:

Don't wait another second to live your dreams.

We often think we must be ready to act , but the truth is we will never be ready while we wait.

We only become ready by walking the path, and battles are seldom won in ideal circumstances.

Money is not the real currency in life , the real currency is time and every second we wait is a second we waste.

Your biggest motivator is the ticking clock and the impending reality that one day it will be too late.

Your biggest fear is getting to 80 and realising you haven't lived, that you haven't done what you wanted in life because of fear.

True regret is a medicine none of us want to taste.

We must decide what we really want, set the bar high , go after it now and accept nothing less.

You deserve respect, but you will live what you expect, this life will pay you any price but it's up to you what you accept.

You must act now from where we are with what we have , right now , not tomorrow or next week , right now.

Take the first step , make the draft plan .

Find out what knowledge you need to make this dream a reality.

Taking action now towards the goal in mind is crucial, if we wait we risk losing the drive to make things happen.

We can never be fully ready because we don't know what exactly is going to happen, a lot of it is learned along the way - especially if you're doing something brand new.

If not, reading what has been done before in your area will give you a good understanding of what might work.

Every second we spend thinking about, instead of acting towards our goal is wasted time.

You cannot afford to wait because if you do not act , someone else will , someone else could also be thinking what you're thinking and act first.

Those who wait for opportunity will wait in vain because opportunity must be created, first in the mind, then in the world.

We cannot see the vast opportunity that surrounds us unless we believe it is there, believe it is possible and act on that belief, at the time it arises.

The world is pliable and opportunities do not wait for people to be ready.

You must become ready on the road.

The obstacles you have to overcome on the move will mould you into the person you need to be to reach your biggest goals.

You must be patient, to be practitioners of who you believe you will be one day.

Getting into the mindset of whoever you want to be right now, because until you become that person in mind, you cannot in body.

As we start acting differently, different actions bring different results and if the new actions are positive and aimed at a certain goal , just like magic the world begins to transform for you, towards the life you wanted.

The leap of faith is acting now, feeling unready aiming for something that may seem unrealistic, but this is an essential leap and test to be overcome.

As the days go on with the goal in mind , it will seem to become more likely and you will feel more ready until it feels definite.

All things are possible but there will be required ingredients to your success you might not know yet, so the first step is to gain the knowledge required.

Once you begin to learn that knowledge you are on the road to your goal.

Organization and optimization of your time will make it easier to be efficient.

If time is the real currency, are you getting good value for what you spend your time doing?

If not , is it not time you used some of your seconds working towards something phenomenal?

You only have so many and it is losing value every day as we age, think about it.

We must create a sense of urgency because it is urgent if you want to succeed in an ever changing world.

If we wait our ideas, products and services may become irrelevant because new technology and innovation is always changing.

Our ideas are only viable when they come ,

Strike while the iron is hot is good advice ,

Success Comes From You

When the ambition and goal is strongest and clearest.

Clarity is essential when pursuing dreams and goals, every detail of your dream should be clear in your mind down to the sights, colours and smells.

When we think about our goal we should feel it as if it's already here, and start acting like it is.

Dress talk and walk as if you are that person now.

Whatever our current circumstances everyone has the ability to build in their minds, set the goal then determine the first step.

If your circumstances are bad there are more steps, but there are steps.

Start from step one and walk in confidence always keeping the big dream in mind knowing that this can happen for you.

We have a waking mind and a subconscious mind.

The subconscious knows things we don't, it is responsible for our gut instinct, which always seems to be right so follow that.

Everyday listening to that voice, keeping a clear vision of your goal in your mind and confidently taking action towards it.

It's possible for you if you act,

But time is ticking.